Electric Firing

Creative Techniques

Electric Firing

Ceramic Arts Handbook Series

Edited by Anderson Turner

The American Ceramic Society
600 N. Cleveland Ave., Suite 210
Westerville, Ohio 43082

www.CeramicArtsDaily.org

The American Ceramic Society
600 N. Cleveland Ave., Suite 210
Westerville, OH 43082

12 11 10 09 08 5 4 3 2 1

ISBN: 978-1-57498-294-7

Publisher: Charles Spahr, President, Ceramic Publications Company, a wholly owned subsidiary of The American Ceramic Society

Art Book Program Manager: Bill Jones

Series Editor: Anderson Turner

Graphic Design and Production: Melissa Bury, Bury Design, Westerville, Ohio

Cover Images: "Spaghetti Jar" by Richard Busch; (top right) "Alligator Plate" by Jayne Shatz; (bottom right) "Birds and Bones" by Kelly King.

Frontispiece: Stoneware platter by Daryn Lowman

Printed in China

Contents

Preface

Electric kilns are a wonderful thing! They're so readily available and relatively simple to install that any artist can take advantage of the incredible potential this tool has to offer. Nearly every ceramic artist I know uses an electric kiln to some extent in their studio to assist them in creating work. They appreciate the control and dependability this type of firing offers in helping them to achieve their desired results.

As the popularity of electric kilns increased within the past few years, studio potters and manufacturers made this tool even more versatile. Here are a few examples of what has been happening:

Electronic controllers: If you don't have one get one. Case closed. Electric firing is about consistency and control and these devices take that advantage much further. They work extremely well and also save energy. Crystalline glazes for example were once the domain of a select few, but now they are simple because of these devices.

Refractory coatings: ITC, a refractory coating material, can be applied to elements and the insides of kilns to give electric kilns even better durability and economy. ITC coated elements can last many times longer and they can withstand reduction firing. I coated the inside of one of my Skutt kilns 10 years ago and it's still going! And Nils Lou, author of The Art of Firing, has done hundreds of firings using a simple bunsen burner under his ITC-coated electric kiln. It works and it works well.

Materials and products: Manufacturers now produce literally thousands of products developed for use in electric kilns. Prepared clays and glazes for all firing temperatures and tastes make it possible to get most any type ceramic body with your choice of color or glaze effect.

In this book we've included information on all these topics and more. Further, we've also included some inspirational stories from artists who are pushing the envelope on how to use readily available materials.

By bringing technical sophistication to the masses, the electric kiln has opened a window to creativity and innovation from unexpected sources and has led to the "democratization" of the ceramic medium. I hope you'll find this book informative and inspiring in your own work.

Anderson Turner

Low-Fire Electric Reds

by David L. Gamble

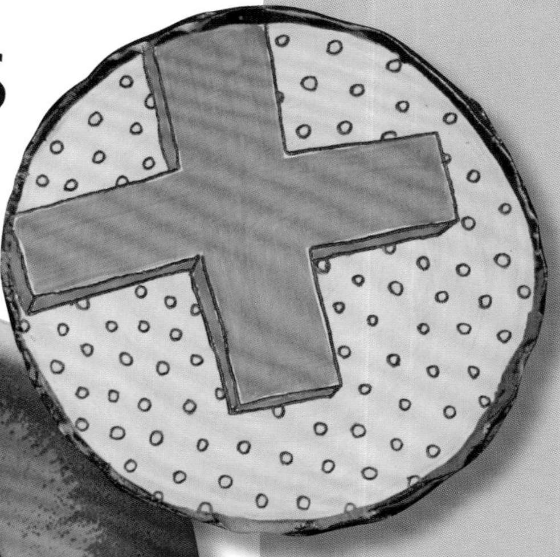

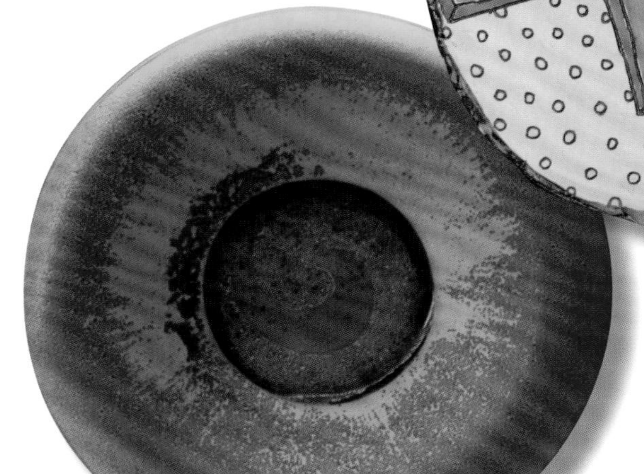

Above: Plate, by David Gamble. Cross is glazed with red underglaze.

Left: Untitled, by Scott Bennett. Amaco LM series Coral glaze with wax and Black overspray. As the wax melts in the kiln, the black moves.

I'll start by explaining there are two different types of commercial red glazes that I normally use. One type is an extremely bright color and harder to achieve and the other is a newer tomato red color that is AP (Approved Product of the Arts and Creative Materials Institute) nontoxic and dinnerware safe. The latter is formulated with inclusion stains, which are continuing to be improved. The color is encased in zircon, which makes them safe to use even in the classroom.

The AP nontoxic reds are extremely stable and were used to create red velvet underglazes that can be fired from cone 05 to as high as cone 10—only salt seems to blush them out.

The success of underglazes has allowed the development of gloss and matt red glazes that have been formulated to work well at the low-fire cone 05 range and other glazes formulated for the cone 4–6 range. These are extremely reliable. Three brushed coats will usually be enough of an application and you get nice tomato color reds at both temperatures.

Bright reds are not dinnerware safe and are extremely sensitive to variations in firing conditions. There have been many times that an art teacher has asked me about the use of these types of red glazes. I understand the space and time challenges that teachers face, but you cannot put these glazes in with your normal glaze firings and expect good results. They are affected by how tight the load is stacked, other glazes (mostly copper greens), and temperature. If you're firing to cone 05, I can almost guarantee there will be problems. The glaze will most likely have variations from clear to gray to black, and if you're lucky, a spot or two of red. Note: Amaco glazes were used in the pieces shown here, however, many companies produce similar glazes.

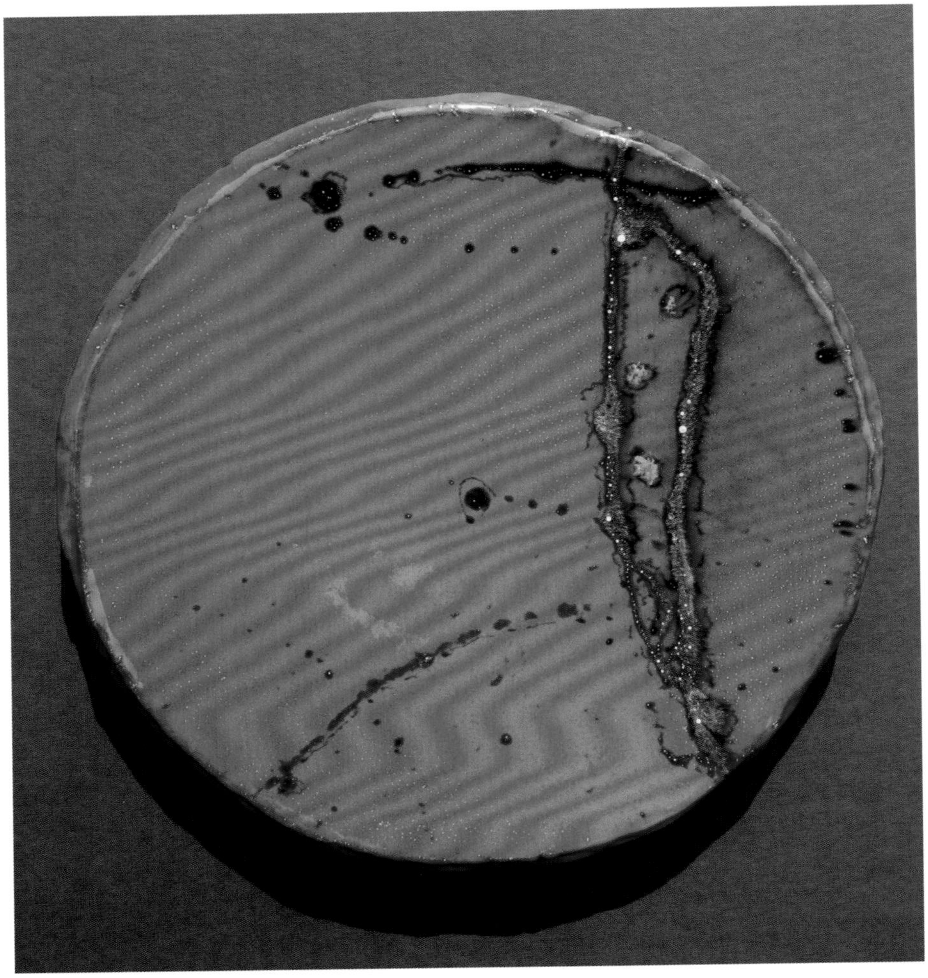

Platter, by David Gamble, glazed with red glaze and blue brush strokes on top.

Process

Here are my suggestions of what you need to know and do to achieve the bright reds!

Bisque your clay body slowly to cone 04 (12 hours to get all the gases out). Although these glazes are not considered translucent, the clay body color does affect them slightly. White bodies will make the glaze appear brighter in color than darker bodies.

Using a brush, apply the glaze thicker than the normal three coats. Four coats will usually work, but too heavy an application may cause the glaze to run. Glaze application may need experimentation and practice.

Load the kiln very loosely. There is a need for lots of space between the pieces for air circulation. I leave the peephole plugs out during the firing, thus allowing extra oxygen to enter the kiln chamber.

"Redhot Chilli Pepper Diner," by Jerry Berta. Glazed with red underglazes.

Do not fire above cone 06 (1828°F), preferably using witness cones for observation. I have been firing at cone 07 (1789°F) with great results. These glazes seem to like the cooler temperatures.

Fire as quickly as you can, four hours is ideal. If your pieces are larger, an example being my 22-inch platters, take them up slowly to about 1200°F. This may help to eliminate cracking problems. Then turn the kiln on high to fast fire to the end of the firing.

More Observations

If your kiln is vented through the bottom with a system that draws air through the top of the kiln, this will help give you more oxygen in the kiln and better red results. Remember that kilns, depending on how they are stacked, may not fire that evenly. This can cause cold spots and hot spots. There can be a difference in temperature equal to a couple of cones from top to bottom—depending where the kiln sitter or thermocouple is located. This variability can really affect bright red glazes. Newer kilns with zone control and multiple thermocouples tend to fire more evenly. If you have an older kiln, place cones in the top, middle and bottom of the kiln so you can keep a record of what happens in the firing. They can help provide answers if problems do occur.

Now that you know the process, I will describe my experimentation with red glazes. I've been placing them on different color clay bodies, layering over glazed fired pieces and layering one coat of gold glaze over the top.

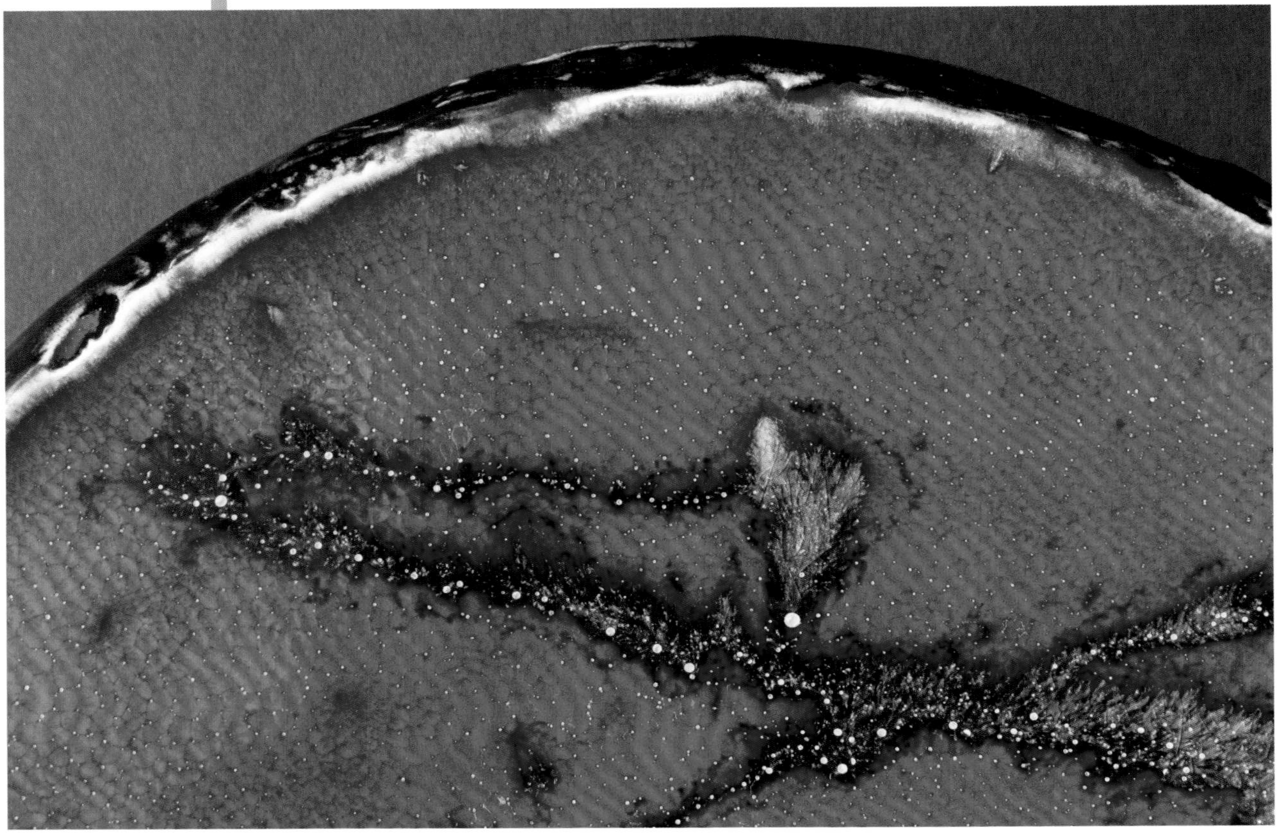

Platter, by David Gamble, glazed with red glaze, blue brush strokes and one coat of gold used for accents.

I then place the pieces next to peep holes to brighten the color or place shelves over the edges to deepen and take away the color. This is what is exciting to me—not getting it perfect, but having the surface color change and vary while having some control over what the changes will be. I am an extreme advocate of using commercial glazes the way a painter would use his tubes of paint. Experiment, test to the "max" and make them your own. Years ago, I was asked to be a glaze doctor at the National Council on Education for the Ceramic Arts (NCECA) in Las Vegas. I agreed, but told them to label me a glaze deviate instead of a glaze doctor.

Don't be afraid to experiment. Don't be afraid to sacrifice a few pieces on the way to discovering something more exciting.

Low-Fire Surface Decoration

by Gail Kendall

Finished plates, approximately 8 inches in diameter, with glazes and luster, fired to cone 03.

Back in the 1960s, only the low-fire process afforded access to a broad range of saturated colors. With various encapsulated stains that have come onto the market, a whole range of reds and oranges have become reliable at high temperatures. I still work with low-temperature materials for philosophical reasons as much as anything else. My goal is to align my work aesthetically to its peasantware ancestors from Europe and Great Britain. One of the aspects of peasant pots that I love is the casualness of construction and glazing that is common to the finished object. Village potters collecting scant remuneration for their labors could not invest huge amounts of time in their work. It's likely that more basic and less controlled firing technologies also contributed drips, splotches, blurring and other variations that add to the overall feeling of freedom that I admire.

Process

First, greenware is painted with White Slip (figure 1). I use brushes with either coarse or soft bristles, depending on the desired surface texture. Small areas missed are allowed to remain. Next, I draw through the slip on the surface (figure 2). I use a sharp knife to cut through the slip to trace the shape of an edge, or create a design or texture. I also may use sgraffito techniques to texture areas

with a stick or pencil, or draw other patterns onto the surface, revealing the red clay under the slip (figure 3). Once the pot is bisque fired to cone 03, I paint the entire surface with a black underglaze—watered down as much as possible but still opaque when applied. After it dries briefly, I wash it off with clean water and a sponge, retaining the black in the recessed details. I let the piece dry thoroughly and then begin applying fields of small, black underglaze dots (figure 4).

I always use a food safe commercial clear glaze on the interior of all soup tureens and teapots, or any other form that may hold liquid. Fashionable or not, I am pleased with my work when it displays a lustrous gloss of just the right thickness and juiciness.

I apply four or five coats of Gerstley Borate Base Glaze in the remaining unglazed areas (figure 5). I enjoy the subtlety of commercial gloss next to my own gloss glazes, which have a softer appearance. I then fire these pieces to cone 03. After the work comes out of the glaze firing, I may add some 24K burnished gold luster to handles, small buttons of clay, or other details (figure 6). This luster is formulated with small amounts of yellow ochre that rises to the surface during the final firing to cone

"Guardian Angel," 11 inches in height, slip-cast earthenware, with underglazes, fired to cone 04.

of dance and being a practicing gymnast herself, accounts for the circus theme so prevalent in their work. Nisha developed her own trapeze troupe at this time, GravityWorks Canada, whose routines she choreographed and took on the road. They started out in Canada, then travelled to the United States, and eventually to Mexico where she took to the air in GravityWorks South. This meant that Dan's beloved Esther literally ran away with the circus and joined up with other elephants, zebras, acrobats and camels, which made their way into the work.

The angel, one of the subjects to emerge from the Ferguson's work after moving to Mexico, once again reflects their immersion into, and

"Zebra Dance," 17 inches in height, slip-cast earthenware, with underglazes, fired to cone 04, by DaNisha Sculpture.

love for, a new geography and culture. Angels are omnipresent in the architecture and art of Mexico, and this is where they established their new home and studio, following the birth of their second child. "After moving to Mexico," Nisha relates, "the first thing that infiltrated my work was the colors of this beautiful country. I find that I am feeling freer to experiment with color in more unusual ways." And that may explain why "Esther" now has a bright yellow sister. "Line, color and composition are my playground," Nisha continues, "and I use them to express everything I feel and see inside my head. Over the years my drawing skills have improved so much, and with each year they continue to improve. It is such a pleasure to be able to render what you feel. I'm always discovering new things and learning more about how to really see. My work is continually evolving and changing.

For an artist having a love affair with brilliant colors, it is difficult to imagine a better place to be than in an old colonial gem of a town in the central highlands of Mexico. San Miguel de Allende exudes color—color in the most surprising of combinations. Just dashing out the door on a routine errand can be an otherworldly experience. All year long, aubergine, copper, peach and scarlet blossoms carpet the streets and form kaleidoscopic drifts along the sides of the road. In the springtime, towering jacaranda trees burst into lavender canopies of shade. Not since watching a kid let loose at an easel in kindergarten will you find houses all in a row painted yellow, cobalt, fuchsia and orchid. Around the arched windows and doorways are found further ornamentation: stencils, tiles and trim colors that enrapture the senses. It is like stepping back into the unedited innocence of a rainy day, armed with a new box of crayons and lots of paper.

The culture and landscape of Mexico has provided so much inspiration for the Fergusons, and yet another source of energy has come in the form of liberation. In the nearby town of Dolores Hidalgo, an important center of Talavera pottery in Mexico, Dan discovered a master craftsman, part of a multigenerational family mold making business. He agreed to produce the complicated, time consuming and demanding plaster piece molds for Dan. How appropriate that the experience of a skilled, competent, Mexican artisan lend a hand to DaNisha Sculpture.

"Sculpture is my department; drawing and painting is Nisha's department. However," Dan reminds us, "design is what unites us. The overall design of a piece is where we collaborate most and it is here that we have had to feel around the most in order to find a purchase with which to climb. It has been slow sometimes, but we feel now that we are beginning to understand the subtle, yet profoundly important rules of elegant design which will help us create something very beautiful and very pleasing to the eye."

Using Majolica Glazes

by David L. Gamble

The recent surge of interest in majolica decorating by contemporary clay artists has prompted the development of specialized commercial glazes for schools and artists. In the traditional majolica technique, coloring oxides are brushed over an opaque unfired white tin glaze and fired so that the colors fuse into the opaque glaze without distorting the decoration. Today, glaze manufacturers achieve the same effect of this colorful technique with their own versions of products, many of which are marketed under different names. When faced with hundreds of glazing choices in catalogs, it can be very confusing to decide which products will be suitable to the task at hand. The distinguishing features of these products are that they will not move and they create a colorful surface ideal for detail work.

Using Majolica Glazes

Commercial majolica products are formulated to be painted onto an opaque base glaze, and typically meant to be fired in the cone 04–06 low-fire range, although many products will also work on top of a cone

Manufacturer's Chart

This chart, though not comprehensive, provides you with an idea of the wide variety of majolica glazes that are available. Studio suppliers often carry several brands, so they are a good source of information about not only the brands listed below but also similar products from other manufacturers. Sample kits comprised of 2 oz. bottles are usually available—a great way to test glazes without a major investment.

Manufacturer	Brand	Colors	Cone	Size
AMACO	GDC's	36 colors	Cone 05–5	2 oz and pints
A.R.T.	Glazewerks Majolica	35 colors	Cone 05–04	4 oz and pints
Duncan	Concepts	162 colors	Cone 06–5	2 oz, 8 oz
Laguna	Creatable Colors	19 colors	Cone 06	pints
	Versa 5	21 colors	Cone 05	pints
Mayco	Stroke and Coats	64 colors	Cone 06–5	2 oz, 8 oz, pints
Spectrum	Majolica/Ultraglazes	66 colors	Cone 06–6	2 oz, 4 oz, 2 oz Super Writers

5 base glaze on a cone 5 clay body. Even though a white base glaze seems to be fine at higher temperatures, problems can arise with black and other colored base glazes because they can cause an the decoration to bubble up.

While the commercial products work best on an unfired base glaze, some also work fine when applied directly on bisqueware, although they may be slightly less glossy without the base glaze underneath.

Majolica glazes can be treated like paints, but there are some differences. Like paint, you can lighten any of them with white, and colors that are close to one another on the color wheel (blue and green, yellow and red) will mix. You can also darken colors. Glazes, however, do not mix like paint in that yellow and blue will not make a nice green. Only through testing will you be able to discover which colors mix and what the results will be. Also most majolica glazes are opaque and are made to stay put—so they do not blend well when layered. If you mix any glazes, do it while the glaze is liquid instead of trying to blend them on the surface of your work.

Testing is important before applying any glazes, Experiment with different base glazes, mixtures of glazes, and different thicknesses as well as thin coats over and under other colors and glazes to help you understand the possibilities and limitations. I've tried using black, blue, red and other colors as the base, glaze including both gloss and

The key to successful majolica glazing is to test what you're doing before working on a piece. Remember that a glaze on a white clay body may look quite different on a red clay body or a dark slip.

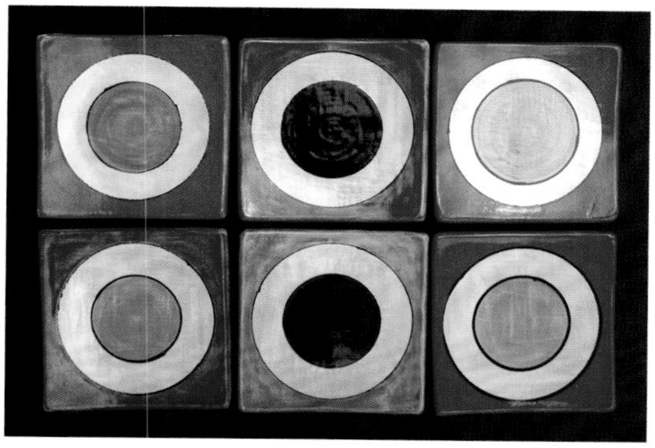

Paper color charts are not that accurate, though they will give you an idea. Actual ceramic chip charts are better but they are usually not on your clay body. These decorated sushi plate tests are two coats of majolica glaze from the each of the manufacturers in the chart. They all become opaque with three coats, so I tried two coats to see how strong the colors were.

matt, with great results. One series or manufacturer is not necessarily better than another, and your tastes will differ from other potters. Consider also convenience and what's available nearby. I've been able to use all the glazes I've tested on my pieces successfully.

Each manufacturer provides instructions on the container and on their websites for proper use of their products. Some may have restrictions on food safety, but generally most should be dinnerware safe when applied and fired according to the instructions.

Jitka Palmer
Narrative Vessels

by Jim Weaver

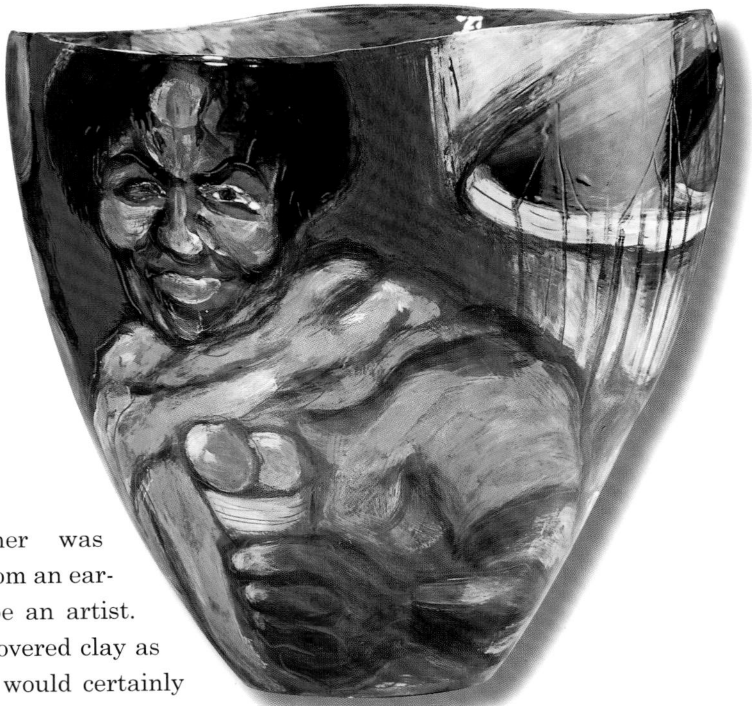

"Hackney Downs," 15 inches in height, coiled and pinched red earthenware with slips, stains, oxides and clear glaze.

Jitka Palmer was destined from an early age to be an artist. Had she not discovered clay as a schoolgirl, she would certainly have found another outlet. She grew up in Czechoslovakia during the 1960s and '70s. When it came time to enter a university, she needed to make a career choice. "My parents wanted me to pursue medical studies," she said, "so I did, qualifying as a doctor of medicine at Masaryk University, Brno, in 1984." The following academic year, she taught human anatomy there. "A year later," Palmer explained, "I married an Englishman, moved to London and left medicine behind to become a ceramics artist." She completed the ceramics program at Croydon College of Art and Design in 1987 and received a British Craft Council grant in 1990 to set up a studio.

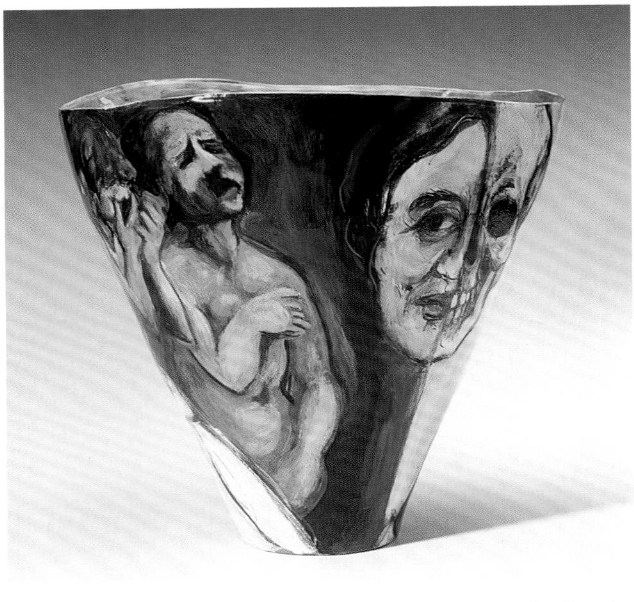

"Florence," 17 inches in height, coiled and pinched red earthenware with slips, stains, oxides and clear glaze, by Jitka Palmer.

Her small vessels are wheel thrown, while the larger ones are coil built. She works in red earthenware, because she likes the effect she achieves when the color of clay shows in her work. Palmer's pieces are narratives based on stories and themes, and she prefers to work on a series of pieces linked by a central theme. "I draw on my personal experiences, past and present, to capture the spontaneity of ordinary human life."

Her narratives generally begin on the outside of the vessel and are completed on the inside, and she attempts to create a visual tension between the two surfaces. "Sometimes the outside depicts the real world while the inside is an imaginary world," she said.

Palmer's figures are painted in quick, broad strokes with finer details left to the viewer's imagination. She uses colored slips mixed with oxides and stains to achieve the desired effect. Before the pieces are initially fired, she outlines the figures and other important elements using the pointed end of a paintbrush. This results in a raised surface along the edges of the outlines and exposure of the red clay beneath the slip. Once fired, her works are covered with a clear glaze and fired again to produce a high gloss.

Palmer keeps a sketchbook where she records images of people she sees while going about her daily activities. She uses the sketches to help her remember particular faces and situations. "I look at them when I need a spark," she explains. "I like to sketch people at work, using their tools." When preparing images for her vessels, Palmer draws and paints on large sheets of paper using ink, dry pastel and watercolor. She sometimes makes clay "sketch bowls," where she experiments with ways to convert flat images to curved surfaces. "I enjoy painting on the curved surfaces," she says, "since I believe it is more challenging and the images are often more dramatic."

PHOTOS: JASON INGRAM

"Slavonic Dances," 16 inches in height, coiled and pinched red earthenware with slips, stains, oxides and clear glaze.

Using Colorful Underglazes

by David L. Gamble

"Teapots" by Jim Kemp. Jim uses a low-fire red clay body and airbrushes underglazes onto the greenware. The last color he applies is black, which is sprayed across the piece to highlight the variations in heights of the surface decoration. The pieces are once-fired to cone 02.

Commercial underglazes are basically clay slips containing colorants, and they're a great way to add color to your work using a variety of application methods. And since they're formulated to have low drying shrinkage, they can be applied to bone-dry greenware or to bisque-fired surfaces. In addition to being able to change the surface color of your clay body, underglazes can also be used to change the texture of the body.

When used to add color to surfaces, underglazes have an advantage in that they are composed mostly of clay with very little flux, so they'll stay put and won't run, which makes them ideal for detailed decoration. While most underglazes were originally formulated for use at low-fire temperatures, most, maintain their color in the mid range and some even as high as cone 9 or 10.

Simple Application

Underglazes can be applied by brushing, pouring, dipping, spraying, sponging—pretty much anything goes. Each application method has different requirements. If an underglaze is too thick for spraying or using as a wash, just add water to thin it down. If it's too thin for silk screening or monoprinting, leave the container exposed to air to evaporate some of the liquid.

Underglazes work best with a clear overglaze, although other glazes of varying opacity and color may also be used. I've had success with whites and very light-colored glazes, but darker glazes seem to muddy or absorb the color of the underglaze. The overglaze can be anywhere from matt to glossy. You'll find the clear deepens the value of the colors regardless of application method. If you're sealing the surface of work that will come in contact with food, be sure to use the appropriate food-safe clear that matches your clay body and firing range.

Applying an overglaze can be tricky. If you've applied underglazes on bisque, you'll find that they'll smear when brushing on a clear overglaze because moist glaze moistens the underglaze. Use a fan brush and float the first coat on without going over the same area twice. Wait for the first coat to dry completely before brushing on a second coat.

I've recently used underglazes to create a watercolor effect by thinning them down and painting them onto a semi-white glaze that is layered over another colored glaze underneath. The colored glaze (sometimes gloss, sometimes matt) melts through the white and gives it a richer off-white look. The clay body is a red terra cotta that can handle a number of multiple firings if needed. I've been creating pieces from my travel sketches to permanently document places I've traveled to in a sketchbook-like manner.

"3 Women Praying" by Debra Fritts. Debra sculpts in terra cotta clay and bisque fires to cone 02. She then covers the piece with black stain and then underglazes are applied, wiped and scraped, then fired to cone 04. She continues with final additions and does a final firing at cone 05.

In this example from my "Sketch Book Travels," series, I bisque fired a clay slab to cone 03 then layered base glazes—3 coats of key lime with white, and 3 coats of low-fire white on top. The sketch is then executed with thinned out underglaze washes and fired to cone 04.

Rimas VisGirda slab builds his plate forms from a terra cotta body. Following a pencil outline, he brushes on underglazes then applies wax to the entire surface. He redraws the figure and the outer border by scratching through the wax and into the clay surface and then inlays liquid black underglaze into the scratched lines. After bisque firing to cone 05, he waxes the figure portion and outer edge again but leaves the background alone. After sketching in flowers with a pencil, he applies underglazes to the flowers, leaves and stems and further defines them with black underglaze. He applies wax over the flower stems and leaves then sponges blue underglaze onto the background. After firing to cone 5, he adds shading with an underglaze pencil then fire to cone 3.

Testing the limits

Through their testing, clay artists have been very influential in the increased use and relabeling of underglazes. When they successfully experimented with firing underglazes above the recommended cone 06 to a cone 5 with little or no change in color, manufacturers relabeled their products to reflect the change. The hobby industry also helped promote higher ranges by developing a line of cone 5 casting porcelain, meaning more potters were working at higher temperatures. Even though the majority of underglazes can survive a cone 5 firing, usually resulting in a more vitreous surface, always test before using them on your artwork.

Through the years, my friends and I have done many tests, taking underglazes to cone 10 in different atmospheres. Many of the underglazes change color and most become very vitreous, even glossy, without a clear glaze over top. I've even fired some underglazes at cone 11 and 12 in Europe with nice results.

At the University of Indianapolis, Dee Schaad mixed some of the new bright red and yellow underglazes into a cone 10 clear glaze in

Paul Wandless paints underglazes on plaster in reverse, painting the foreground first and the background last. He then pours a low-fire white slip on the plaster. This picks up the underglaze image and inlays it into the clay. After bisque firing to cone 02, he applies a thin clear glaze then glaze fires to cone 04.

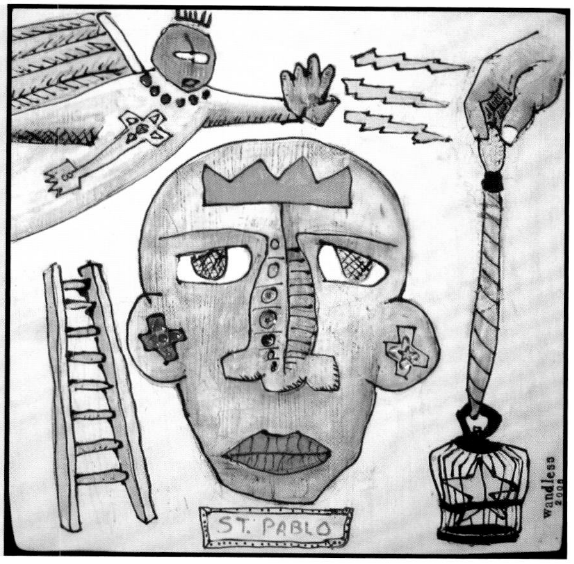

Tom Meunick uses white stoneware or porcelain then bisque fires to cone 06. He then uses underglaze pencils to draw on the surface. After drawing, he atomizes it lightly with water then applies a glaze by dipping or spraying.

Steve Howell uses a body made from half porcelain and half raku clay. After the initial bisque firing, he adds underglazes and bisque fires again. Because a higher bisque absorbs less smoke, he bisque fires cool colors to cone 06 and warm colors to cone 04. After the bisque, he places the piece upside down in a 2×4-foot brick pit in sawdust layered with copper carbonate, salt and bits of sticks and wood, then covered with a Kaowool blanket.

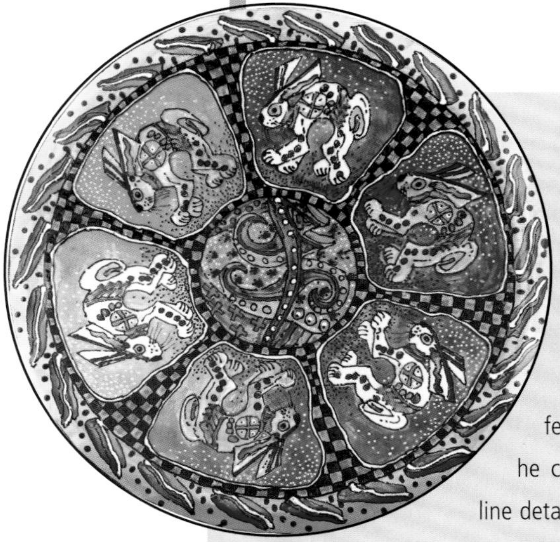

Ron Korczyski bisque fires a white low-fire clay to cone 04 then applies underglaze by brush on the bisque piece. He uses many underglaze colors in different size applicators that he can squirt out and draw line details and dots of color. The final piece is fired to cone 05.

Scott Rench silk screens images he creates on his computer. Images are screened onto the clay while it is still wet so it can later be shaped. After bisque firing to cone 04, Scott airbrushes a clear glaze and fires again to cone 04.

a ratio of three parts clear to 1 part liquid underglaze. He then brushed the mixture on top of various cone 10 reduction glazes, including a temmoku, with great results—the bright colors stayed bright. When potters told me that the new bright reds that fire to cone 10 blush out to white, it made me wonder if mixing them in a clear glaze would help protect them from the salt when salt firing. Experimenting with all these colors allows you to find new and unexpected results when testing in, on and under anything you have on the glaze shelf.

One thing to remember, however, is that if you're using underglazes at a higher temperature than recommended, things can change. One clay artist using a black underglaze at cone 10 noticed that the next pint she opened looked the same in the jar but had a very greenish cast when fired. The company told her they had to reformulate because of government regulations and material availability and reformulated the color to fit their cone 06 to 5 suggested firing temperatures. The higher cone 10 temperature was overlooked and not taken into consideration.

Kesl and Tilton

A Collaboration

by Don Pilcher

Plate, 11 inches in diameter, wheel-thrown earthenware, with commercial glazes and underglazes, fired to cone 06.

Each winter, John Tilton and Lennie Kesl have put aside their usual studio pursuits, and turned their minds and imaginations toward a compelling collaboration. The product is a large group of painted plates, cups and jars. The appeal of this work reveals itself at several levels, as does the content. This is the work of two serious artists making the most of their talents and experiences, in concert. As it turns out, each is also a musician and, in both endeavors, they cook.

Tilton has been a well-known potter for a long time. His most widely recognized work features organic porcelain forms with unbelievably beautiful glazes, many of them of a unique macrocrystalline variety.

Kesl is irrepressible and inexhaustible; in the course of his life he has been many things: a member of the 30th Infantry Division that invaded Germany in World War II, a Fuller Brush salesman, a drummer, a recording vocalist on three LPs and a CD, a painter, a sculptor, and an art professor. He and Tilton began their collaboration while both were teaching at Santa Fe Community College in Gainesville, Florida

The pots they make employ the techniques of commercial ceramic production but they also utilize the methods and sensibilities of fine studio pottery. The colors, glazes and kilns are exactly what you'd find at the local greenware/paint-your-own-pottery shop. But the clay is custom blended by Tilton, who also throws all the "blank" forms that Kesl paints. Like his own work in porcelain, Tilton's blank pots hide his hand. The vessels are smooth, symmetrical, uncomplicated and perfectly suited to carry Kesl's images. Unless you know about undercuts and wall thickness, you wouldn't know that these pieces aren't cast or jiggered.

The yearly collaborations between the two last up to six weeks and the product is divided equally. For the most part they keep the work in their own collections, occasionally loaning a group to be exhibited locally. Tilton will sell a piece once in a great while. Kesl's are not for sale.

While both these men claim to be somewhat reclusive, you can't go anywhere in Gainesville with them and not be greeted by well wishers. Their fame as artists and musicians precedes them. Tilton is part of the Hot Club de Ville, which plays a monthly gig in town. Kesl sometimes joins them as a vocalist. But their love of music is not limited to public performances.

In preparing the studio for this collaboration many years ago, the first thing Tilton installed was a first-rate sound system. The music plays for long stretches. The selections are an eclectic mix but favor Django Reinhardt, Stephane Grappelli, and the composers and lyricists of the great American standards.

While the music plays, Kesl offers a captivating, free-association dialog on all matters: art, music, friends, foreign languages, world history and gems from his personal experiences. Today Kesl is wearing one of his father's dress shirts. Consider that for a moment.

Kesl was born in Edwardsville, Illinois, in 1926—the same year as Miles Davis and Marilyn Monroe. As a young man, he met and was befriended by the sculptor, David Smith, and box/collage artist, Joseph Cornell. But in the main, Kesl's insights about art are informed by his knowledge of music. Pitch equals value and volume equals intensity. In his world, the black hair on his figures is chosen because black sets the pitch for the orchestration of all the other colors. When discussing his compositions, he recommends we consider the interstices, the intervals. Look closely at the color and textural modulations that separate his shapes. His color mixing and application are a kind of phrasing, sometimes subtle and sometimes impetuously exaggerated. There is nothing postmodern, academic or pedantic about his commentary or his painting. All of his images, processes and theories are fluid and affirmative. This day, Kesl is painting thirteen plates, the largest being 24 inches in diameter. Each carries the face of a young woman. Each face is viewed straight on, each head selectively proportional and comfortably composed within the circle. The exactness of the plate's rim complements the nuanced irregularities of the hair.

He paints slowly, precisely, reflectively. As he paints he recites a line from Henry David Thoreau, "Man is a tool of his tools" and then he turns a phrase about the nature of his subjects, the young girls, finding them to be "virtue on the hoof." One of Kesl's signature moves is the use of the underglaze bottle caps to impress cheeks and, sometimes, teeth. We are left to decide if this is a droll improvisation with the tools at hand—Thoreau—or a kind of shorthand not seen anywhere else in the work. It's hard to know, but good art always raises a few questions. And in these pots we are reminded of the difference between talent and art. Talent applies itself and fills some space. Art, as seen here, goes in through our eyes and informs our minds. If it's really good, then it lives in our hearts.

This investment of talent, time and money raises the question "Why?" For each of these men, it's the art. Tilton believes that this is work that should get made. And it needn't be burdened by the demands of the marketplace. There is no rush to product. While he is in the business of being a potter year round, he also is wise enough to know that some of the best parts of life aren't bought or sold.

Kesl simply loves to work. And he loves to work with Tilton, in the hope of making magic. As mentioned before, Kesl keeps his share of what he makes. He is a true collector—of many things: drawings, paintings, books, ceramics, LPs, correspondence and photos. Yet he is quick to note that we won't be pulling the material world up through a hole in the clouds to heaven. The greatest truth is that the two of them, to use the old jazz expression, "really cook."

"Elephant Bowl," 14½ inches in diameter, wheel-thrown stoneware, with commercial glazes, fired to cone 06.

Plate, 10¼ inches in diameter, wheel-thrown earthenware, with commercial glazes and underglazes, fired to cone 06.

Kesl says that working with Tilton is like making sure-fire fudge. By his own admission, he doesn't know that much about ceramics—but he doesn't need to. This is a seamless team effort; no duplication of skills, no necessary steps avoided.

There are serendipitous moments in this partnership and they occur with such frequency that it's difficult to choose just one to retell. But here it is, and it stands for many others, all equally moving.

As a storyteller, either in song, prose or paint, Kesl has a legitimate gravity in his delivery. His voice is a seasoned baritone; some notes round, some thin, some with a little sand, some with a little gravel. His diction and phrasing are poetry, period. This afternoon he is playing his own CD, Mood Swings, and singing along with himself as he paints. The first cut is "You Stepped Out of a Dream" (Herb Brown and Gus Kahn, Leo Feist, Inc.) and the lyrics ask:

Could there be eyes like yours,
Could there be hair like yours,
Could there be teeth like yours,
Honest and truly?

Kesl's brush moves in ballad time and he lifts it to sustain a phrase. The song ends with, "safe in my arms, here in my heart."

Moments later, his thoughts turn to the long-ago death of a friend. As he shares their story, his eyes tear and his voice hesitates. He stills his brush for just a moment and looks down at the thirteen young faces on his plates, each looking back at him. He collects himself and resumes the process of painting life into each countenance. Perhaps this is one of those moments when intellect and intuition appear at the same time. It seems like a little bit of magic. Kesl finishes his story with a gentle but penetrating stare. Then he reminds all around, "You can't be a passive listener."

Nor should we be passive viewers. It is not often that we come across a full body of mature work that has remained relatively unknown; especially work made for over twenty years. This partnership and these pots provide us with a rare look at a sustained involvement of like-minded, knowing and passionate individuals.

The Depth and Complexity of Underglazes

In addition to Kesl's composition and imagery, there is a good deal about the underglaze and glaze application that accounts for the success of these pots. Unlike the figurative ceramic works of Picasso or the village potters in Mexico, whose work is primarily single stroke, Kesl builds the color over days of patient application. In this particular series, he has incised the features and then added as many as twenty layers of color over a spattered ground, not unlike stucco. Sometimes he thins the color, other times he applies it like cake batter. In two instances, he applied dried out and crushed underglaze like chopped nuts to a freshly painted pool of contrasting color. The result is a complex and vibrant pastiche that responds with satisfying intensity to the later application of glazes.

This is not an inexpensive undertaking; Tilton has assembled an amazing quantity of pigments. Including underglazes and glazes (a clear, and several brilliant yellows, oranges and reds), they have nearly 500 jars of color on hand. They go through the catalogs together and Kesl decides how many of each color he wants. And there are new ones yet to try. Tilton brushes three coats of clear for the glaze firing. Each piece is fired at least twice and as many as four or five times until the image is right.

A word about the firings: Tilton brings a commitment to detail that might never occur to some of us. For example, when using self-supporting cones, he uses a bubble level to set the shelf so that the cone is always true to level for each firing—tight-is-right. And he fires the cones by visual observation so that the potentially fugitive cadmium-selenium hues don't escape. This seems like a throwback in this age of programmed firings, but it's a practice typical with labors of love.

Plate, 14½ inches in diameter, wheel-thrown earthenware, with commercial glazes and underglazes, fired to cone 06. All pieces are wheel-thrown by John Tilton, and glazed by Lennie Kesl.

Collaborative Escape

by Anne Tilton

Central to making sense of the John Tilton-Lennie Kesl collaboration is the fact that their temperaments are complementary. On the face of it, they are opposites. John is reserved; Lennie is flamboyant. John makes pots that don't show the hand; Lennie, as a courtesy to the viewer, makes rudimentary efforts to conceal his hand, but actually wants the viewer to see where he has been (to see, as he told John once, "how you've suffered"). Musically, John prefers to be in the background, playing rhythm guitar; Lennie likes to be in the foreground as a vocalist. When they divide up the pots after a working session, John and Lennie often want completely different pieces. These complementary inclinations help their partnership function smoothly.

Less obviously, they have strong similarities. Artistically, both men are strategists. John, with his mathematical background and love of solving problems, is a more obvious strategist, and the desire to conceal his hand in the collaborative pieces demonstrates this. Lennie's painting, which at initial impression might appear carefree and spontaneous, is deeply and strategically considered, with the composition paramount and each mark made with great deliberation and concentration. Both men also have a strong work ethic. After a short conversational period when Lennie first arrives for a session, they plunge into their work for days on end. Both revere historical works and reference them in their own work, if somewhat obliquely. John's pottery "blanks" have their roots in great functional pottery, and Lennie constantly uses specific references in his work. I remember one instance in which he was painting two birds flying toward one another across a plate, the birds' beaks nearly touching. Pointing at the nearly-touching beaks, he turned around and said, "That's God touching the hand of Adam on the ceiling of the Sistine Chapel."

One reason for the lack of commerce may be that their sessions together serve as an escape from their normal lives. Lennie is "cocooned" with us. He is fed good food, sleeps in quiet and beautiful surroundings here, is shielded from interlopers and is shepherded through the flow of the pottery-making process by John (who truly fills the Good Shepherd role). Thus insulated from the concerns that normally invade his life, Lennie can live for a short, suspended time reveling in pure claywork. If Lennie's experience is perhaps more tranquil than his day-to-day life, John's is more stimulating. Used to working alone in porcelain, John switches to working in red earthenware, giving Lennie the run of the studio, and being bombarded with ear-blasting music and running commentary all day long. He comes away from their collaborative sessions feeling that (although his eardrums may have been damaged) his right brain has been stimulated and his horizons have broadened. If their working together were to become a commercial enterprise, the "escape from daily life" factor would be lost.

Incidentally, the Gypsy Jazz music that they love, which was popular during WWII, may play a part in the "escape." In the 1940s, with the War grimly raging, people would leave their cares behind and dance to this music in the dance halls of Paris. It's possible that Gypsy Jazz music, which is experiencing a resurgence in popularity today, promotes that feeling of freedom from boundaries.

Scott Bennett
Craft on Craft

by Glen R. Brown

"Harelip Platter," 13 inches in diameter, thrown and altered earthenware, with commercial glazes.

Despite their common classification under the rubric of craft, the professions of ceramics and jewelry-making have rarely been coaxed into relationships more profound than polite cordiality, the mutual well-wishing of disciplines with common goals yet markedly different constitutions and personalities. In the field of contemporary jewelry, clay is regarded as a rather ignominious material—one that generally requires the support, literally and figuratively, of a more enduring metal. In contemporary ceramics, jewelry rarely exercises any kind of persuasion over form or technique, let alone conceptual concerns. In contrast to the influences exerted by sculpture or even painting, that of jewelry on claywork is nearly nil. The paradox of this situation—that two canonical craft disciplines might be less conversant with and sympathetic to one another's central concerns than either is with those of the supposedly more distant field of art—has provided sculptor Scott Bennett with the impetus for a series of work that combines the skills of handbuilding, throwing and glazing with a focus on issues of display that are generally of greater concern to the jeweler than the ceramist.

Bennett's intention is decidedly not to produce ceramic jewelry. The inflated scale of his works is sufficiently daunting to disqualify them as anything even remotely intended for adornment of the body. Nor could his sculptures be said to represent standard forms of jewelry in more than the most abstract manner. The pieces of his "Big Jewelry" series are indeed visual disquisitions on rings, brooches and pendants—jewelry types that in their ubiquity and ancient lineage could be compared to the ceramist's primal form, the vessel—but they display an obvious interest in the conceptual nature of these types, rather than the utilitarian aspects of their construction or even the formal problems that they present to the designer. Bennett is intrigued by the symbolic aspect of rings, especially in the context of certain human emotional re-

"Two-Prong Pearl," 9 inches in height, earthenware, with commercial glazes and gold luster.

"Four-Prong Pearl," 6 inches in diameter, earthenware, with commercial glazes and luster.

lationships and the standard social practices, such as engagement and marriage, that circumscribe them. His organically suggestive sculptures are inspired by the libidinal dimension of the body, and are intended to convey through their form something of the instinctual drives that, at an obscure level of the psyche, exert their influences over some traditions of exchanging jewelry as gifts between the sexes.

Above all, Bennett's colossal ceramic jewelry forms are committed to exploring the practice of display, in particular those aspects of display that are conveyed by the word "frame." To frame something in a conceptual sense—an argument, for example—is to ready it for presentation by imposing upon it certain recognizable conventions of form. The frame as a physical object, as in the context of a painting, is as much a signifier of the interpretive system through which the framed object can be read as it is a more mundane device for protecting that object from potential knocks, abrasions and other pernicious consequences of its material existence.

Bennett's works, however, suggest that the concept of the picture frame—which insinuates itself in the experience of all paintings, whether their inclination is to simulate the depth of field glimpsed through a window, to deny that field by assuming an ineluctable flatness, or to break completely from the limitations of a field by escaping the frame—is less relevant to the aspect of display in ceramics than is the framing function of the bezels, channels, prongs or other settings in jewelry.

It is telling that Bennett's "Big Jewelry" evolved out of a narrower focus on the gemlike properties of translucent glazes and the sense of preciousness that they can bestow on objects fashioned from common clay. Several years ago he began a series of "Double-Lipped Bowls" in which these characteristics would come to the fore and establish a precedent for the framed elements of his later abstract jewelry sculptures. A potter by training, but a sculptor by inclination, he arrived at the grommetlike form of the "Double-Lipped Bowl" by throwing a vessel on the wheel and experimenting with extreme disproportion between the three principal elements of foot (which diminished considerably), body (which nearly disappeared) and lip (which came to dominate the vessel to the degree that it effectively inverted the essence of that form, making it more about mass and surface than containment).

"To make one of those forms," he explains, "I started with a large container, pulled the wall up, necked it in, then brought the lip back out. After cutting it off the wheel, I would flip it over and drop it onto a plaster dome form I'd made. That gave it a concave upper surface. It also trapped air, almost like an inner tube, although it wouldn't always actually be sealed."

The lip would then be drawn down over the form and flared out. What

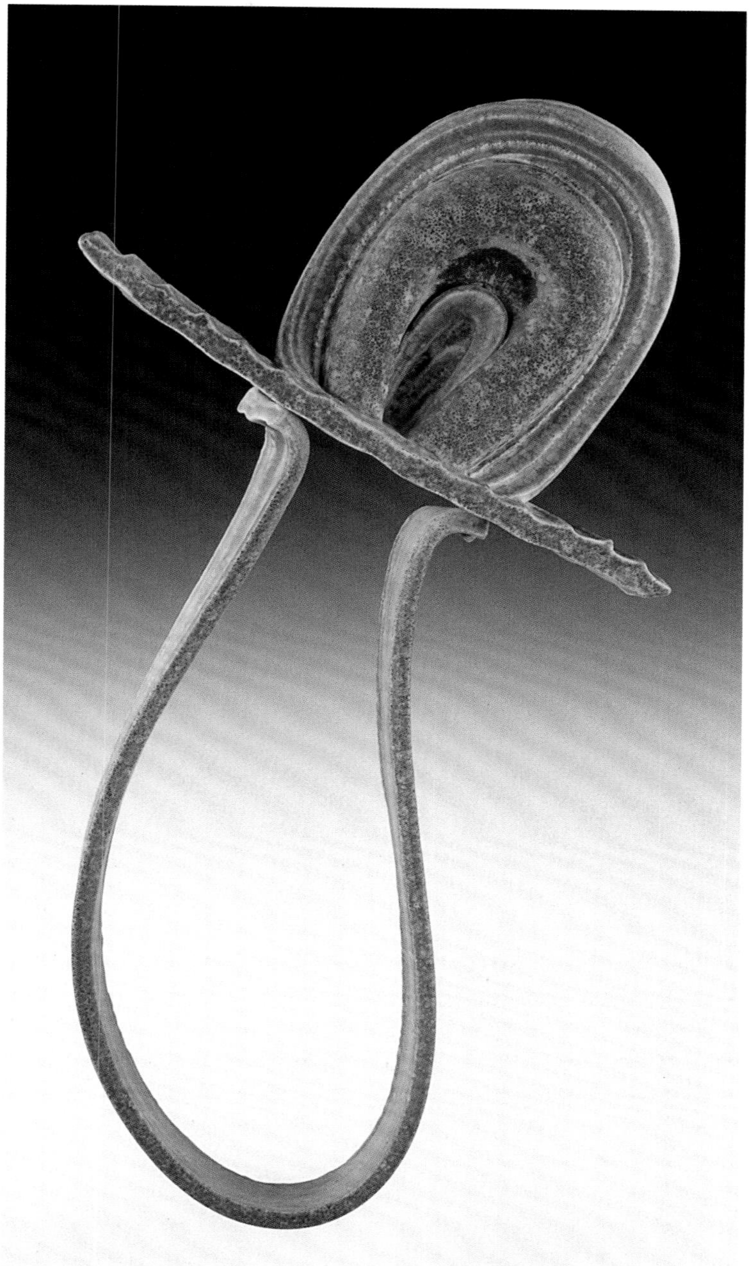

"Jewel," 20 inches in height, thrown, altered and assembled earthenware, with brushed and sprayed commercial glazes.

made the final shape so significant was the fact that the majority of its surface, like that of a low bowl, ended up moving laterally away from the vessel's center, but did so while creating the impression of convexity as much as concavity. The result was an unexpected affinity with cabochons as well as containers, a condition that would eventually lead Bennett to treat his forms as huge gems to be situated within gigantic jewelry settings. In part, this shift in orientation away from the vessel and toward a more purely sculptural format was influenced by frequent encounters with jewelry at the art fairs where he sold his work.

"The shapes were made to sit as a bowl would sit," he explains. "I started hanging them on the wall because when you show your work at art fairs you get a lot of questions like, 'What do I do with it? What's it for?' They were just decorative shapes that happened to be thrown on the wheel. By putting them on the wall I did get people away from looking at them as bowls. Then I got inspired to make pieces that were specifically wall pieces, like reliefs."

Contemplating the ways in which the method of presentation influenced the experience of the work, Bennett began looking more intently at the jewelry on display in the booths near his own. Arranged on presentation boards rather than worn on the body—removed, in other words, from their utilitarian context as ornament—the brooches, pendants and rings that he encountered seemed more properly diminutive examples of relief sculpture. What might happen if one were to expand the scale of these forms? The question was particularly intriguing because the glazes with which he was then experimenting had already begun to suggest to him the polished surfaces of gemstones.

Process

Bennett's glazing method in the "Double-Lipped Bowls" series entailed covering the terra-cotta surfaces with a white engobe, then brushing on as many as five coats of low-fire commercial glazes. Over these, he sprayed a thin layer of magnesium carbonate to achieve a matt effect, plus a variety of other glazes to produce haloes and blushes. Finally, as in "Fat-Lip Bowl," he generally brushed a wax resist onto the entirety, then sprayed the surface with a glossy black glaze that tended to bead up yet cling to the wax as it dried. During firing, the black glaze pitted through the matt glaze below, creating a spotted effect as well as a palpable texture. "It's like a bleeding crater," Bennett observes. "Clay people think that I'm using stoneware and doing some heavy iron reduction, but it's just the result of experimenting with glazes."

In a variation of this technique—notable in "Harelip Platter," —he added several coats of clear glaze to the surface before applying the wax and spraying on the glossy black. During the firing, the clear glaze caused the black to run, producing a

"Fat-Lip Bowl," 18 inches in diameter, thrown and altered earthenware, with commercial glazes, by Scott Bennett.

streaky effect similar to the veining in semiprecious stones.

End Process

Bennett's burgeoning interest in jewelry led him to embark upon a systematic analysis of those basic elements composing the objects of the jeweler's craft. Imitating these on a larger scale in clay, he began to situate his double-lipped forms within open compositions vaguely suggestive of rings, brooches and pendants. Duplication of the visual aspects of jewelry was not so important to him as approximation of the impression that certain jewelry creates on the viewer. Focusing on the psychology inherent in the display of gemstones, he began to extrapolate from this a content of human significance that transcended the narrower context of jewelry. "As I looked at more and more jewelry," he remembers, "I started noticing that the setting sometimes rivals the stone, and it's almost unclear which is more important. Some jewelry seems to reflect a lust, an obsession with a really precious object. Showcasing that object becomes the primary aim, and the setting becomes really lavish. The whole thing ends up as a fetish. It verges on greed."

The cynicism of this conclusion is not, of course, directed at jewelry per se, but rather at a general human weakness that tends to infect the experience of preciousness and render it inseparable from an irrational desire. For this reason, Bennett has endeavored to make his "Big Jewelry" pieces simultaneously alluring and somewhat unattractive, "elegant and almost ugly at the same time," like the conflicted elements in the obsession with preciousness itself.

This contradiction, the tensions between the beauty of an object and the corruptive power of the impulse to possess it, is the true content of his sculptures. The image of jewelry is merely a heuristic device, and Bennett could easily exchange it for another. "I've thought," he says, "about making a piece that's a really elaborate button, a magic button that you could push but that you're not supposed to touch. It would be maddening. There's something that may be just outside your reach, but you've got to have it. It could be a number of things. Who knows? That's a large part of what my works are about."

Clearly, Bennett could have explored this theme without drawing inspiration from jewelry making, but the fact that his references to this sister craft are so unexpected in ceramic sculpture adds an important dimension to his exploration of desire. The perception of hierarchy between art and craft is generally irritating to ceramists, but the anomalous character of Bennett's sculptures suggests that, in part, the foundations of this hierarchy can be uncovered in attitudes within the crafts themselves—in the aspirations that each craft discipline has for achieving the status of art and the relative lack of interest that it displays in emulating the concerns and practices of other crafts. The very strangeness of Bennett's "Big Jewelry" is its strength. Craft imitating craft is nothing new, but it has become much rarer in a contemporary context in which desire for treatment as art is so often the driving force behind the work. Bennett's work suggests that true risk-taking and the consequent discoveries it offers are perhaps more readily available to the ceramist, not in casting off the mantle of craft, but in precisely the opposite strategy—in seeking inspiration in the conceptual concerns of the fellow craft disciplines.

V'Lou Oliveira
Iconoclasm and Wit

by Andrew Phelan

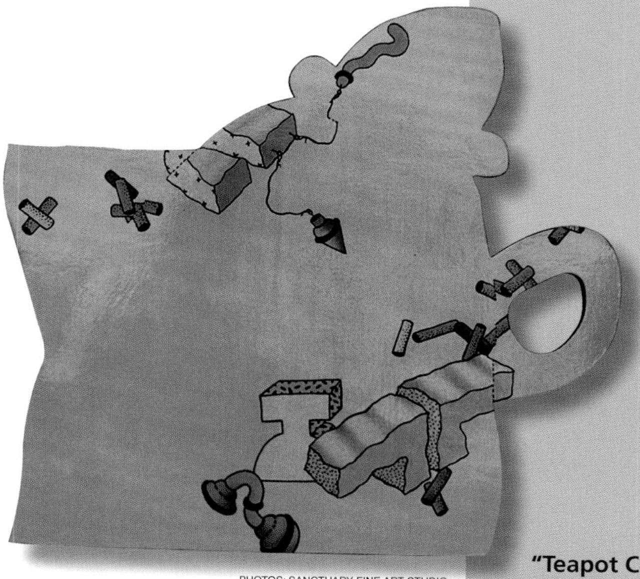

PHOTOS: SANCTUARY FINE ART STUDIO

"Teapot Cutout," 12 inches in height, slab-built white earthenware, with underglaze pencil and glazes, fired to cone 06.

Oklahoma is a young state, less than a century old, but it has a long tradition of excellent ceramics artists. Native Americans, populating the area prior to statehood, had a rich ceramics tradition stretching back to approximately A.D. 1000, and examples of that period found in sites such as the Spiro Mound in eastern Oklahoma give eloquent testimony to the rich and varied wares produced under a highly developed, sophisticated social structure. However, within a few decades of the opening of the Indian Territories in 1880, European settlers began to appear in what would soon become the state of Oklahoma. Among the early 20th-century ceramics artists who became influential were John Frank and Roger Corsaw. Their impact on the state and the region was remarkable, and the state developed a thriving group of potters and ceramics artists working in a variety of styles and traditions, combining functional pottery in the English tradition with a strong Native American representation. More recently, these have combined with still another, very contemporary tradition of nonfunctional ceramics. For the past quarter century, there has been a strong presence in the state emanating from the direction of the West Coast.

That presence is embodied in California native, but longtime Oklahoma resident, V'Lou Oliveira. Oliveira is one of those artists who maintain traditions by expanding them. She has significantly shifted the focus of ceramics in Oklahoma toward the West Coast clay tradition. With her longtime commitment to pop art and popular culture, dating back to her time in graduate school, Oliveira's work has consistently focused on the iconographic imagery of popular culture. She has varied her focus during her career, but has always come back to seeking and finding her inspiration in objects of popular culture, such as pink flamingo lawn decorations, Chia Pets and other forms of kitsch.

V'Lou Oliveira prepares to glaze a plate in her studio.

Educated at California State University, Humboldt (B.A.) and the University of Washington (M.F.A.), Oliveira came to Oklahoma in 1977, following a short stay in Texas. She has been teaching at the University of Oklahoma ever since, and has built a reputation in the region as both a teacher and artist.

Oliveira's witty, nonfunctional pieces reflect her California heritage and her education under Howard Kottler, Patti Warashina and Robert Sperry. She began breaking away from the functional tradition in ceramics early in her career. "While I started out as a potter, I was never very good at it. I did some slip casting as an undergraduate, and then

"The Lonestar State," 14 feet in length, slip-cast white earthenware, with cast and altered edge bricks, fired to cone 06.

slab building in graduate school." One of the first shows she entered was an invitational exhibition of teapots, where she decided to submit an entry that would poke fun at the concept—a "Teapot Cutout." For a few years, she explored this and other equally outrageous interpretations of teapots. Following the teapot series, still working within the confines of a flat plane, she embarked on a series that investigated various states in ceramic format.

Shifting gears in the late '90s, Oliveira began a series of nonfunctional vessels and brightly decorated plates and platters. When one of her dogs died, she made a crematory urn in the dog's image and then embarked on making a series of these urns that doubled as containers for dog biscuits. Decorated with scenes from the happy life that faithful Fido led, these containers were designed to bring back the happy memories. She sent the resulting works to the "Art Show at the Dog Show" in Wichita, Kansas. However, these failed to elicit much interest. "Everyone thought the idea was sick," Oliveira recalled. Nonetheless, drawing on the dog concept, she began working with dog motifs. Following the urn series, she began a series of plates and platters also using dog imagery. These met with a more favorable response and she received an award for "Robo Dog." The iconoclastic, witty, sardonic approach that has become a hallmark of Oliveira's career continues to be reflected in her current work and is

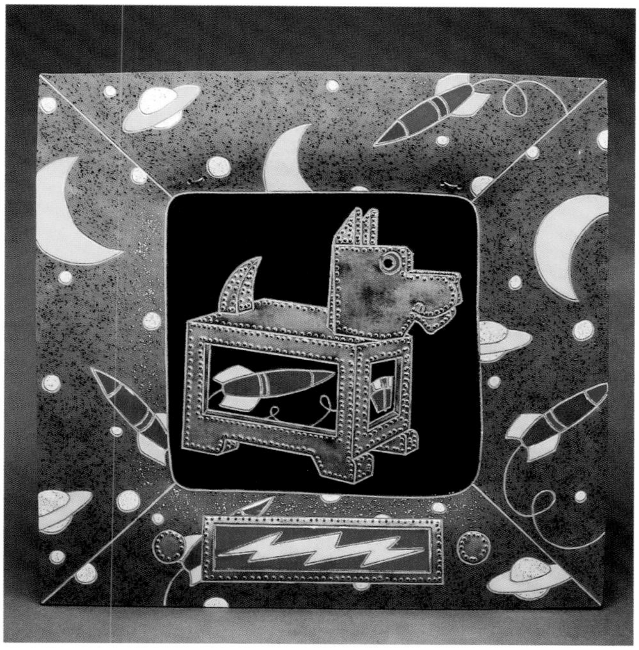

"Robo Dog," 20 inches square, drape-molded and carved terra cotta with glaze.

"Deco Japan Terrier" with commercial dog figurines, 19 inches in diameter, drape-molded and carved terra cotta with glaze.

not only a result of her own creative personality, but also reflects her aesthetic heritage.

Oliveira worked as Kottler's graduate assistant shortly after he moved into the "funk" scene. While the tradition he had learned at the Ohio State University and Cranbrook did not completely disappear, it manifested itself through the use of unorthodox images, nontraditional materials and a distinct lack of functionality. Oliveira embraced that vision and it has continued to be a fundamental motivating factor in her work.

She begins with a sketch or drawing and plans the design of each piece prior to beginning work on the final piece. "I did a lot of printmaking and drawing in undergraduate school, so I feel most comfortable in making my images on paper and then transferring them to clay." Describing herself as "nontechnically oriented," Oliveira is much more interested in the end result, and will appropriate techniques from nonceramic fields. This attitude was reinforced by both Warashina and Kottler.

For the last few years, her work has focused on brightly decorated wall pieces with painted and incised decorations and similarly decorated large platters. The platters are rolled out on a slab roller, draped over a mold, then put on a potter's wheel for the addition of a thrown foot. These results have references to mid-20th-century popular culture. Visit her house and you will discover the source for her current work—mass-produced Japanese-export ceramics from the pre–World War II era. These "trinkets," individually decorated in bright, painterly glazes, are slip-cast dogs, cats, bunnies, etc., and are displayed by the dozens on numerous shelves.

She says the three dogs she shares her house are "insane," but her passion for the dogs, as well as for the Japanese pop-culture motifs, are reflected in many of her new plates.

She traces her interest in the pre–World War II Japanese-export ceramics to Kottler. "He would drag me along when he went antiquing. He was always looking for pieces to add to his now-famous art-deco Noritake collection. He was quite obsessive about collecting, so we went out looking very often." Not only has Oliveira been collecting these pieces for years, but she has devoted considerable time to researching them. She recently gave a presentation on the topic at a conference on popular culture in Albuquerque, New Mexico. In this age of appropriation, it is interesting to note that the Japanese, in producing this export ware, adapted images from Czechoslovakian and German ceramics and then exported them back to the West.

Oliveira's time studying with Warashina and Kottler coincided with a period of great fecundity and rethinking of the ceramics tradition. However, while the connection to a long tradition appears tenuous, it does survive. Warashina studied (albeit briefly) with Shoji Hamada, the legendary Japanese traditional ceramist, during his five-week visit to the University of Washington in 1963. That same year, however, Warashina drew greater inspiration from her exposure to Rudy Autio, who filled in for Sperry while he was on sabbatical in Japan. Autio's influence is more easily discernable in her work and Warashina began exhibiting "funky" pottery shortly after Autio's stint.

Oliveira's work is usually made with one of two clay bodies—Trinity Ceramics' White Modeling Clay or Armadillo Clay's Longhorn Red. These bodies give her the ability to achieve the bright luscious colors she uses.

Consistent with the iconoclastic approach that has characterized her entire career, she uses commercial glazes. She fires her bisqueware to cone 05, then keeps her glaze firings in the cone 06–07 range, in order to keep the brilliance of the colors.

She ruefully mentioned that, with some of the new health and safety concerns, she has been having problems getting colors she likes and, unfortunately, a number of her favorite colors have disappeared. However, she has proven to be enormously resourceful in the past and it seems certain that she will find the means necessary to fulfill her creative visions as they develop.

What lies in the future for Oliveira is unclear, but almost certainly her incisive wit and appreciation for underappreciated aspects of popular culture will lead her in directions uniquely personal. We will be richer for her efforts.

"La Petite Chien, Fifi," 20 inches square, drape-molded and carved terra cotta with glaze, by V'Lou Oliveira.

Pennsylvania Redware

by Denise Wilz

PHOTOS BY LISA SHORT

Pennsylvania Redware platter, 12 inches in length. The design was created using a sgraffito technique then bisque fired to cone 04. Selected areas were then glazed with a green copper oxide glaze then overglazed with a commercial clear glaze and fired to cone 06.

Pennsylvania German folk art found me when I was searching for a different direction to take my clay work. To me this art embodies the spirit of a people who loved life, with their oft-used representations of hearts, tulips, birds and the flower urn. And while the Pennsylvania German potters made mostly plain functional ware with local red earthenware clay, I fell in love with the slip-decorated pieces with their beautiful rich red-and-yellow coloring.

There are basically two styles of decorated Pennsylvania Redware: sgraffito ware and slipware. For ideas to use for decoration, I find inspiration in the Pennsylvania German decorative arts, such as antique redware, fraktur and painted furniture to name just a few sources.

Sgraffito Ware

Sgraffito ware is simply red earthenware decorated with a layer of white slip that is then scratched away to reveal the red clay underneath. To begin, roll out a slab of clay large enough for your mold (figure 1). For this plate I rolled the clay 3/8 inch thick using 3/8-inch dowel rods on each side of the clay as a guide.

To create different-size circles, use a disc cutter that has an arm with multiple holes. Place a needle tool in the appropriate hole, then swing the arm in a circle to cut the clay (fig-

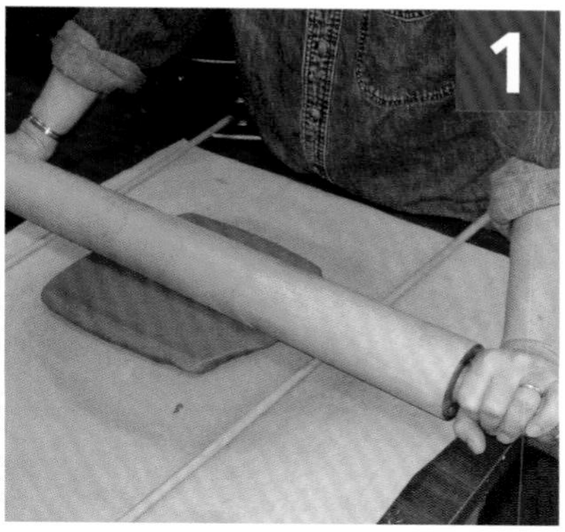

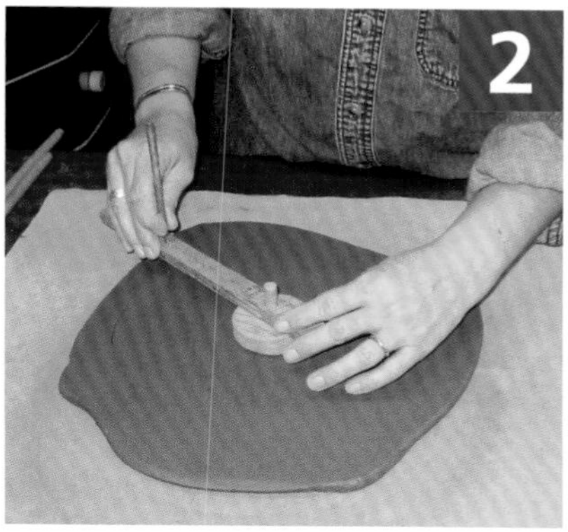

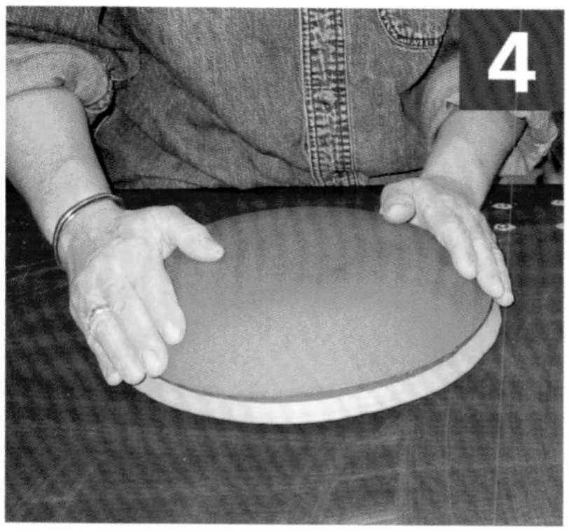

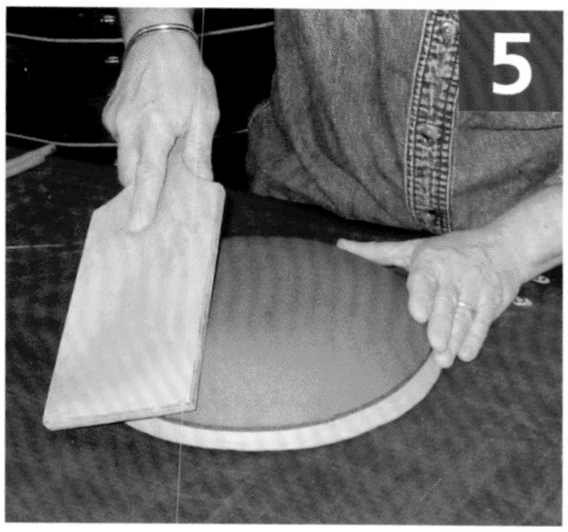

ure 2). Lightly wipe the clay with a damp sponge to smooth the surface.

Center the mold upside-down on the clay circle (figure 3) and carefully flip everything over, using the interfacing or a ware board to aid you. Avoid bending the clay in the opposite direction. Press the clay to the mold with your hands (figure 4); and paddle the clay down as well (figure 5). Smooth and press the clay to the mold by wiping the surface with a damp sponge, then allow to dry to leather-hard.

The Pennsylvania German potters used upside down bowl-shaped molds carved from wood with a foot underneath, which resembled a mushroom. My drape molds are made of bisque-fired earthenware and I use commercially made serving bowls as slump molds.

Remove from the platter mold when it is leather hard and place it upright on your work surface or banding wheel. Apply slip with a 2-inch hake brush (figure 6). Brush on two or three thin even coats of slip, making sure the red clay cannot be seen through the surface. Clean the edge of excess slip and use a coggle wheel to decorate the edge (figure 7).

Allow the slip to dry to leather-hard before you begin the sgraffito process. I use a calligraphy pen with a rounded scratch nib and a stylus for my sgraffito work. Deciding when to sgraffito the piece depends on how

TIP

Roll out slabs on heavy-duty intefacing rather than canvas as it avoids having to remove the canvas marks. Even though interfacing has a much shorter lifespan, I consider it a good trade-off.

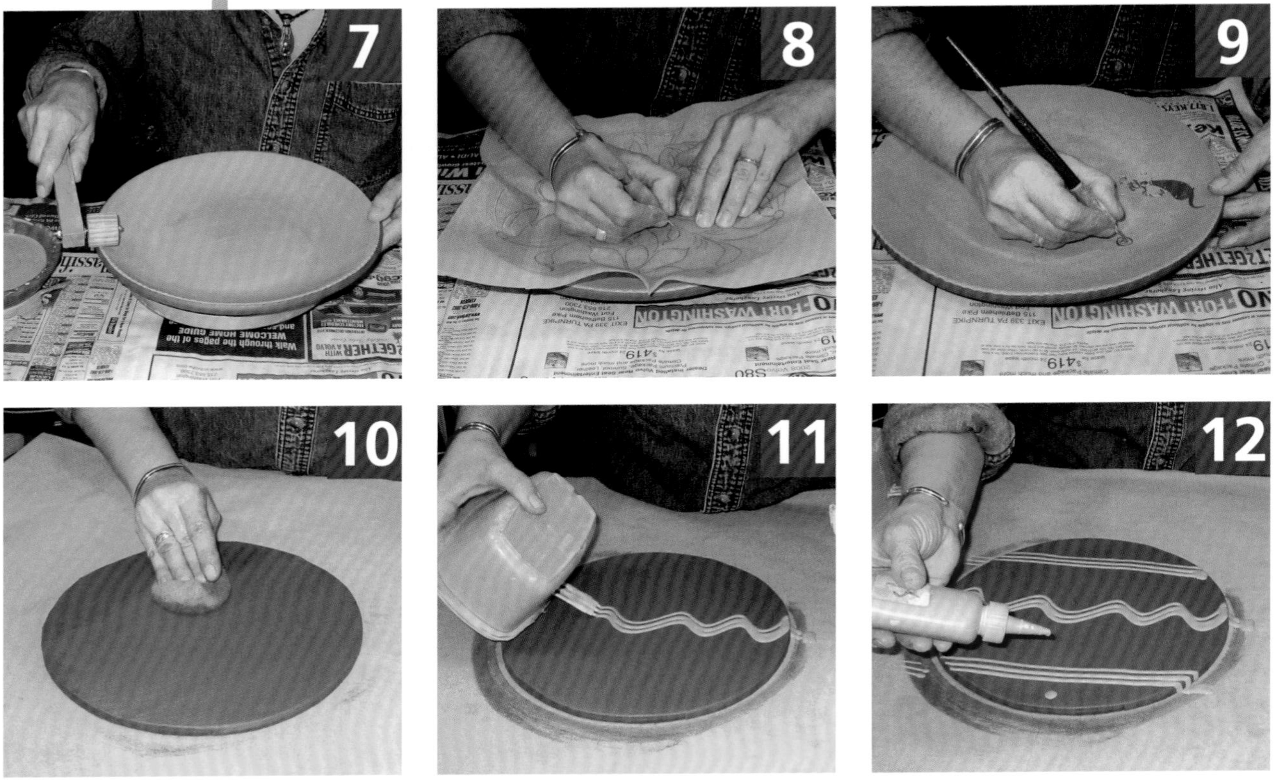

wet you like the slip. I prefer a leather-hard surface but some potters prefer to sgraffito right after the slip has been applied and others like to sgraffito when the slip is bone dry.

You can use other tools, like a wire-loop tool, sharpened stick or even a pencil in a pinch. As for getting the design onto the plate, it can be freehanded with your sgraffito tool, drawn directly on the slip with a pencil or transferred using tracing paper. To use tracing paper, first draw the design onto the paper, making sure it will fit the size of the plate you are making. Center the design on the plate and lightly draw over the design with a stylus or pencil (figure 8) to leave a slight indentation in the slip as a guide. Then use the sgraffito tool you prefer to scratch the design into the slip' revealing the red earthenware beneath (figure 9).

The Pennsylvania German potters applied the glaze directly to the green ware and once-fired the work in a wood-fired kiln. I bisque fire to cone 04, apply a commercial clear glaze then glaze fire to cone 06.

Slip Trailing

Another form of Pennsylvania redware consists of red earthenware decorated with lines and dots of slip. Create a form using the same techniques as described above. To make a smooth surface to work on, lightly wipe the clay with a damp sponge

> **TIP**
>
> Use a high-quality brush to avoid losing bristles in the slip, which can mar the work.

Here is the first coat on a tile mural project. Care has been taken to keep colors from overlapping since most china paints are not intermixable.

One of the advantages of china paints is that the colors are the same before firing as after.

blot with a stencil brush or a small piece of foam rubber. Traditional china painters use a wad of cotton in a piece of silk. Another technique, called pouncing (used to get intense, even color), is done by coating the area to be painted with a sticky oil, and dumping dry powder on with a shaker or mop brush. The excess is then knocked or blown off.

Painting on a slick surface is quite different from painting on absorbent bisque or raw glaze, but one big advantage is that you can wipe it off and start over. Tools made of foam, rubber or wood work well to remove color in selected areas.

Some Advanced Techniques

When I need to spray china paint for a large, even color area, the water-based medium on a slick surface is a problem. So I first spray the area with a fairly thick solution of cornstarch and water, then dry it with a hair dryer. When a solution of color and water is sprayed over this, it stays without beading up.

I also silk-screen china paint. You can silk-screen any substance that will go through your screen as long as it will not dry quickly and if you can mix it to a consistency similar to mayonnaise. You can't print one color over another without firing in between, but you can print colors next to each other. To do this, you will need a medium that will dry fairly hard in a reasonable time, but will still wash out of your screen when it's dry. Potterycraft used to make a product in a tube that was perfect for this, and I've tried many other substances as a substitute. For single colors, ethylene glycol works well, but it never dries, so you can't put a screen down on it for a second color. I'm now using a mixture of water and gum arabic, about half-and-half, and then I mix in dry powder to get the right consistency.

Silk-screening must be done on a flat surface, but printing on tile is just like printing on paper, except for the substance you put through

Colors are often applied in layers. Here the mural has had more china paints applied to add intensity and shading then fired a second time.

"Reef," Humuhumu detail.

"Reef," 6½ feet in height by 14 feet in length. China-painted tile.

the screen. Take a class or buy a kit to learn how. For printing on non-flat surfaces, you need to make decals. Commercial ceramic decals are made using china paints.

I use a process for making screens that's manufactured by Hun-Speedball, and available in art supply stores. It's a light-based system, but doesn't require a darkroom or careful control of water temperatures. Instructions come with the chemicals, and it makes screens that are usable with either water or oil. I use 12XX mesh screen, which is a medium mesh size.

WARNING: Since china paints melt at such a low temperature, there is much less silica and alumina in them than in low-fire glazes. This means that harmful things like cadmium and lead are less bound up in the glaze, so china paints are definitely not for food-contact surfaces. All the precautions for ventilation and dust are doubly important, and they are not for children. There are lead-free china paints available, but most do contain lead. Some even contain arsenic.

Under heavy daily use, china paints will wear off, as they have on your grandmother's everyday china, but for decorative objects and tile, even in showers, the durability is fine. If you want faster, cheaper firings, brighter colors, and more painterly effects than even low-fire glazes or underglazes produce, go as low as you can go—try china paints.

Joan Takayama-Ogawa

China Paint and Lusters

by Judy Seckler

"Rose Parade Float: Tea Time at Great Aunt Tillie's," 9¼ inches in height, slab-built and wheel-thrown whiteware, with china paints and lusters, fired multiple times.

When Joan Takayama-Ogawa, then dean of studies at the Crossroads School in Santa Monica, California, first signed up for a ceramics class on summer vacation, she had no idea it would reconnect her with her past.

What she discovered that summer was that her father's family had a role to play in her newfound creativity. Her ancestors produced ceramics in Tokoname, Japan, for six generations, and several had earned reputations as noted potters in their time. One such ancestor, Jumon I, had a reputation for making red clay teapots and became renowned in several cities for it. This talent for claywork lay dormant in her genes until it was given a chance to bubble up to the surface and lay the groundwork for her new life as a clay artist.

When Takayama-Ogawa swapped the life of a middle-school administrator for ceramist, she chose the

"Tea Totem #1," 22 inches in height, wheel-thrown whiteware, with china paints and lusters, fired multiple times.

teapot as her vehicle. It's a familiar cultural symbol that allows her to express wit with texture and color.

Much of the appeal of teapot art, given its associations with hearth and home, is that it's accessible to the public, who, disarmed by the functionality of the form, are receptive to the message an object contains. Exhibition curators suggest that these messages can range from the complexly autobiographical, to political and to social commentary.

One of Takayama-Ogawa's earlier pieces, "Rose Parade Float: Tea Time at Great Aunt Tilly's," consists of a homey English cottage and intricate flower-garden images that overshadow the actual teapot function. With some of the artist's other works; however, the teapot form is instantly recognizable.

Takayama-Ogawa is known for scholarly explanations of what she does. Despite this, she thinks of her art or an emotional level as well, describing it as "beauty and humor holding one another in check."

Her teapot ideas start with the writing process. Often working from 5 A.M. to 8 A.M., ideas start to flow on paper. Then she takes time to walk the dog. Back at her journal, she edits her thoughts into a concrete idea for a ceramic piece. Her eye often sets out to create provocative pieces in which tension between the forms brings out the most visual interest.

Over time, Takayama-Ogawa has interwoven Japanese and women's themes and even political events into her work. In her "Sea Urchin" teapot series, she covered the pieces with recognizably spiny forms by squirting glaze out of a condiment squirt bottle. The sea urchin texture gave the teapot and its matching teacup new visual interest.

Other series have explored women's domestic role in the kitchen and included stacked tea sets Takayama-Ogawa calls tea towers.

"Coral Tea Set," 12 inches in height, wheel-thrown whiteware with pencil texture, china paints and lusters, fired multiple times, with slab base.

If the tea towers remind the viewer of something, it is because the artist was inspired by the daily chore of stacking dishes in the sink. "Tea Totem I" exists as a largely vertical piece that begins at the base with a teapot, followed by a plate, a smaller teapot and another plate, with three teacups balanced on top.

In one of her series, Takayama-Ogawa looked to the world of pop culture for inspiration, fashioning teapots in the style of women's handbags. These "Teabags," as she calls them, were inspired by the popular television show "Sex and the City." As a devoted fan of the show, she has designed the teapots to reflect handbags the show's characters would wear. The objects fall into three subgroups—trophy, beaded and floral.

The trophy handbag "Blue Gator Tea Bag" evokes the character of Miranda through the classical alligator textures and the whimsical use of the reptile's gold metallic head and tail. A successful, witty corporate lawyer who dresses conservatively on the job, Miranda waits until after business hours to express her unique fashion spirit. Shades of red, orange, blue and purple, as well as exotic jewelry and accessories express her character's duality. The teabag's alligator theme is a reminder of hunting (a sport popular with the powerful set Miranda works among) and

"Ark of Paradise," 27 inches in width, handbuilt whiteware, with china paints and lusters, fired multiple times, with semiprecious stones and gold beads.

a sly reference to the skin that once provided women with so many elegant and luxurious accessories.

The beaded teabags recollect the days of glamorous evening wear, bedecked with multicolored crystals offset by constellations of color. These have the character of Samantha written all over them. A public-relations consultant, Samantha has an appetite for men that oozes from her every pore. By day, she dresses in sleek power suits; by night, her wardrobe becomes sultry. In Samantha's world, most one-night stands look like fun and inspire her lust for life in the bedroom and the boardroom. It is no accident that some of the beaded teabags have gold metallic lipsticks, combs and Mont Blanc pens protruding from the clasp. And the teabag itself looks as though it has enough room for an extra pair of Samantha's panties and a toothbrush. Takayama-Ogawa doesn't mind if her audience also connects with the piece's underlying sexual messages.

The surfaces of the floral teabags have lush tropical flowers spilling over their surfaces or used as accents fanning out from them. The powerful female sexuality expressed in these works speaks to preppy Charlotte's character. She is a former art dealer now involved in public service and charity work, and is always classically polished, poised and perfect. Her outfits are always feminine and often accompanied by a classic strand of pearls.

The character of Carrie is represented by some of the smaller evening teabags, with gold accents and a field of miniature rosettes covering the surfaces. She's a columnist covering New York City's night life. There's a saucy edge to her clothing that mirrors the singles scene she follows. Whether she's decked in spiky heels, a feather boa or vintage wear, she's out to attract attention.

Like the television program that inspired this work, Takayama-Ogawa takes her audiences on a journey, exploring social issues and cultural identity. However, beyond the beautifully textured surfaces of her teapots lie other messages. "Japanese American Cultural Baggage" shows the artist's cultural leanings and contains symbols of her ethnic identity. A teabag fashioned with a bamboo handle, a gold lid in the shape of a stylized fan and a horizontal clasp, patterned after eaves from a Japanese temple, sit serenely on a lacquered tray. The teabag's surface draws its inspiration from the constellation of stars seen in the foothills of Pasadena, California.

The tray is filled with objects like a Medal of Honor commemo-

"Blue Gator Tea Bag," 18 inches in height, handbuilt and cast whiteware, with china paints and lusters.

"Japanese American Cultural Baggage," 28 inches in width, slab-built whiteware, with china paints and lusters, fired multiple times.

rating the Japanese American 442 Regimental Combat Team and 100th Battalion (the most decorated military units in U.S. history), cherry blossoms, rice balls and fans. Also displayed are an origami gold crane; fish to represent those who earned their living by fishing; ginko leaves to represent those who became gardeners to support themselves; and geta, the wooden sandals that were part of traditional Japanese dress. Takayama-Ogawa has cleverly arranged many objects and managed to squeeze in a short history lesson in the process. Meanwhile, the joy of creation has never left her. "Opening the kiln after a firing is better than any Christmas morning," she said.

"Deco Beaded Tea Bag," 9 inches in height, slab-built whiteware, with china paints and lusters, fired multiple times, with semiprecious stones and pearls, by Joan Takayama-Ogawa.

Low-Temperature Multi-firing

After rolling slabs, Takayama-Ogawa slams them on the ground to release moisture. It pools along the outer edges where it can be easily removed. She uses patterns to duplicate forms, a trick she borrowed from the fashion department at Otis College of Art and Design, where she teaches English and speech classes.

It takes between eight and nine firings to create a finished piece. She begins with the highest glaze firing at cone 05 and works down to the lowest at cone 019. She mixes her own glazes, and makes hundreds of test tiles to obtain the color combinations needed. Her teapots have an air of elegance due to her liberal use of gold. The metallic finish is usually the last firing and the most tricky. "You either get gifts and kisses from the kiln or clay breaks your heart," she said. About 50% of her pieces are damaged or ruined before they make it through the entire process.

Versatile Recipes
Engobes, Slips, Glazes, Self-Glazing Clays

by Gerald Rowan

With my work equally divided between sculpture, painting and clay vessels, I thought it would be best to standardize my kiln firings to two cone levels: cone 06 and cone 6. This would allow me to bisque earthenware and stoneware as well as glaze fire earthenware all at the same time—an efficient use of both kiln space and energy.

My preference is to work with vitreous engobes rather than glazes, primarily because engobes can be applied much like paint. Usually two coats applied with a soft brush yields good coverage. I also find I have a greater degree of control with a brush, as opposed to dipping or pouring; however, the recipes here could easily be dipped or poured to meet others' working habits or individual tastes.

I found that the following engobes work well over a wide range of temperatures and are forgiving enough to be used for large vessels and sculpture

Versatile Cone 06–6 Engobes

Recipes

Glossy Engobe 200

Cone 06–04

Whiting	8.9 %
Custer Feldspar	11.1
Pemco Frit 25	50.0
Kaolin	9.0
Silica	21.0
	100.0 %
Add: Bentonite	3.0 %
CMC	1.0 %

Matt Engobe 201

Cone 06–04

Ball Clay	16.0 %
Whiting	9.0
Pemco Frit 25	15.0
Kona F-4 Feldspar	50.2
Kaolin	9.8
	100.0 %
Add: Bentonite	3.0 %
CMC	1.0 %

For each engobe recipe, dry mix all ingredients; add water and allow to stand overnight. If necessary, readjust water content before using.

Color variations of the engobes are possible with the addition of 10–15% commercial stain or the following oxide/stain combinations:

Enamel White

Tin Oxide	5.0 %
Zircopax	7.5 %

Majolica White

Tin Oxide	10.0 %

Off White

Titanium Dioxide	10.0 %

Medium Blue

Tin Oxide	4.0 %
Cobalt Oxide	2.0 %

Opaque Blue

Tin Oxide	5.0 %
Cobalt Oxide	2.5 %

Blue Gray

Tin Oxide	1.0 %
Cobalt Oxide	0.5 %
Iron Chromate	3.0 %

Blue Green

Tin Oxide	4.0 %
Black Copper Oxide	2.0 %
Chrome Oxide	3.0 %

Turquoise

Cobalt Carbonate	0.5 %
Copper Carbonate	3.0 %
Fluorspar	5.0 %

Warm Gray

Cobalt Oxide	0.5 %
Manganese Carbonate	0.4 %
Pink Stain	1.5 %

Dark Brown

Tin Oxide	2.0 %
Manganese Dioxide	3.0 %
Red Iron Oxide	5.0 %

Cone 6 Oxidation Slips and Glazes

With electric kilns, one method of obtaining the subtle nuances and breaks in color associated with other atmospheres is through the use of various slips. Applied in combination, even with simple glazes, they can dramatically alter the typical surface and color. Capable of affecting surface results through texture, intense (oxide-saturated) color, and fluxing the glaze to cause it to run off high spots and pool in depressions, the following cone 6 oxidation slips are designed to be applied on bisque.

Recipes

Vitreous Black Slip

Cone 6

Borax	9.1 %
Nepheline Syenite	22.7
Georgia Kaolin	22.7
Kentucky OM 4 Ball Clay	22.7
Silica	22.8
	100.0 %
Add: Cobalt Oxide	0.9 %
Copper Oxide	4.5 %
Red Iron Oxide	4.5 %

Without glaze, this recipe produces a slight sheen at cone 6; as a raku slip at cone 06, it produces a "ghost" because of the borax content.

Redart Slip

Cone 6

Lithium Carbonate	10.0 %
Spodumene	10.0
Cedar Heights Redart Clay	80.0
	100.0 %
Add: Red Iron Oxide	2.0 %

Blackbird Slip 1

Cone 6

Barnard Clay	50.0 %
Cedar Heights Redart Clay	50.0
	100.0 %

Glassy Slip

Cone 6

Lithium Carbonate	94.5 %
Bentonite	5.5
	100.0 %

To yield runs, apply thinly under or over a glaze; works well with stiff opaque glazes. Color variations may be achieved with the following additions:

Blue	
Cobalt Carbonate	1.5 %
Green	
Copper Carbonate	5.0 %
Tan	
Red Iron Oxide	7.0 %
Opaque Tan	
Rutile	10.0 %

Glassy Iron Slip 1

Cone 6

Gerstley Borate	90.5 %
Bentonite	9.5
	100.0 %
Add: Red Iron Oxide	90.5 %

Blackbird Slip 2

Cone 6

Wollastonite	10.0 %
Barnard Clay	90.0
	100.0 %

Blackbird Slips 1 and 2 may also be employed as a stain without a glaze.

Glassy Iron Slip 2

Cone 6

Magnesium Carbonate	90.0 %
Bentonite	10.0
	100.0 %
Add: Tin Oxide	50.0 %
Red Iron Oxide	50.0 %

Both Glassy Iron Slips should be applied thinly under or over a glaze to yield running; they also are good with stiff opaque glazes.

Glassy Rutile Slip

Cone 6

Pemco Frit 25	81.8 %
Kentucky OM 4 Ball Clay	18.2
	100.0 %
Add: Rutile	81.8 %
CMC Gum	5.5 %

Thin applications of this slip under or over a glaze will cause running; it is particularly good with stiff opaque glazes.

Blackbird Slip 3

Cone 6

Borax	34.0 %
Wood Ash (unwashed)	33.0
Barnard Clay	33.0
	100.0 %

Apply on raw clay as a stain, as well as on bisqueware as a slip.

Recipes

Rutile Slip

Cone 6

Whiting	23.1 %
Kona F-4 Feldspar	15.4
Cedar Heights Redart Clay	53.8
Kentucky OM 4 Ball Clay	7.7
	100.0 %
Add: Rutile	7.7 %

Gritty Terra-cotta Slip

Cone 6

A.P. Green Fireclay	80.0 %
Cedar Heights Redart Clay	20.0
	100.0 %
Add: Chrome Oxide	1.0 %
Red Iron Oxide	4.0 %

For more texture, 10% fine grog may be added to the recipe.

Gritty Yellow Slip

Cone 6

Cornwall Stone	2.0 %
A.P. Green Fireclay	40.0
Cedar Heights Bonding Clay	39.0
Cedar Heights Redart Clay	13.0
Kentucky OM 4 Ball Clay	6.0
	100.0 %

To increase texture, add 10% fine grog.

Medium Brown Slip

Cone 6

Whiting	4.8 %
Albany Slip	67.2
Cornwall Stone	28.0
	100.0 %
Add: Red Iron Oxide	5.6 %

Boiling Slip

Cone 6

Cryolite	24.1 %
Lithium Carbonate	24.1
Wood Ash (unwashed)	24.1
Bentonite	3.6
Kentucky OM 4 Ball Clay	24.1
	100.0 %
Add: Granular Manganese Dioxide or Ilmenite	1.2 %
Rutile	24.1 %

Spring Hill Slip

Cone 6

Dolomite	10.5 %
Ferro Frit 3124	10.5
Nepheline Syenite	22.1
EPK Kaolin	37.9
Silica	19.0
	100.0 %
Add: Tin Oxide	5.3 %

For color variations, add the following oxides:

Blue	
Chrome Oxide	1.1 %
Cobalt Oxide	3.2 %
Green	
Chrome Oxide	8.4%
Cobalt Oxide	1.1%
Gray	
Chrome Oxide	2.1 %
Cobalt Oxide	1.1 %
Red Iron Oxide	3.2 %
Orange	
Red Iron Oxide	8.4 %
Rutile	5.2 %

Off the Shelf Slip

Cone 6

Cornwall Stone	42.8 %
Ferro Frit 3110	28.6
Kentucky OM 4 Ball Clay	28.6
	100.0 %
Add: Any Commercial Stain	42.8 %

The following two simple glazes work well in combination with the preceding slips:

Fat Glaze

Cone 6

Fluorspar	11.2 %
Cornwall Stone	88.8
	100.0 %
Opaque White	
Tin Oxide	6.0 %
Green	
Copper Carbonate	3.0 %

Wally Glaze

Cone 6

Wollastonite	35.3 %
Kona F-4 Feldspar	35.3
Kentucky OM 4 Ball Clay	29.4
	100.0 %
Add: Zinc Oxide	14.1 %

Color variations are possible with the following additions:

Blue	
Cobalt Oxide	2.4%
Green	
Copper Oxide	2.4%
Tan	
Rutile	5.9%
Opaque	
Tin Oxide	3.5%

Cone 08-6 Self-Glazing Clays

Self-glazing clays, among them Egyptian paste, are mixtures that incorporate soluble glaze-forming materials in a porous, open, refractory body. As an object made from self-glazing clay dries, the soluble glaze materials migrate to the surface as water evaporates from the clay. On firing, these materials, visible as a surface scum, melt into a glaze. with the evaporation of the clay body's water.

Because the migration of soluble materials is important to this type glaze formation, the colorants added should also be water soluble, when possible, to enhance color intensity. (Soluble materials may be toxic, so avoid skin contact by wearing rubber gloves.)

White Egyptian pastes usually fire from cones 08 to 05, self-glazing clay bodies can be formulated to fire roughly between cones 08 and 6. Near or above cone 6, these clay bodies tend to melt into a glaze, depending on the length of the firing cycle.

When self-glazing clay bodies are fired at mid-range temperatures, the resulting colors from metal oxides, carbonates and chlorides are increasingly more muted and subdued. At higher temperatures, commercial stains produce better color than do raw metal colorants, and can be used in quantities up to 12%. Self-glazing clays are typically short (low in plasticity) and therefore are best formed by either handbuilding or molding; but they lend themselves well to a variety of firing methods: raku, pit, saggar, reduction, salt glazing and fuming. Also, when clay bodies of this type are used in combination with other clays, a portion of the soluble material penetrates the surrounding clay and produces a "ghost" when fired, which in itself can be attractive.

When mixing self-glazing clay bodies, add 25-30% (by weight) hot water to a lidded plastic container. Add the soluble materials and the colorants and mix well to dissolve; then add the rest of the materials and mix in the container. Any drying that occurs in storage will cause the soluble materials to migrate to the top of the container and form a scum that may be difficult to remix with the clay body. Allow self-glazing clays to sit for several days after mixing to maximize their plasticity.

Because the materials in self-glazing clay bodies are water soluble, they cannot be wedged on an absorbent surface without losing a portion of the glaze formers to the wedging block. If wedging is necessary, wedge on a nonporous surface such as a Formica countertop.

When handling dry greenware, be careful not to chip or rub off the surface scum that has formed, for this is what will become glaze. If self-glazing clay is allowed to dry on a nonporous surface, no evaporation will take place through this surface; therefore, the bottoms of forms dried in this manner should not have deposits on them and will not need to be sponged or scraped.

The following recipes (next page) are suitable for experimentation.

Recipes

Self-Glazing Clay

Cone 06-2

Bicarbonate of Soda	4.0 %
Soda Ash	4.0
Ferro Frit 3195	8.0
Cedar Heights Bonding Clay	52.0
Silica (200 mesh)	24.0
No. 1 Silica Sand	8.0
	100.0 %
Add: Bentonite	3.0 %

Self-Glazing Clay A

Cone 2-6

Bicarbonate of Soda	4.0 %
Dolomite	4.0
Soda Ash	4.0
Whiting	4.0
Cedar Heights Goldart Clay	25.0
6 Tile Clay	23.0
Silica (200 mesh)	26.0
No. 1 Silica Sand	10.0
	100.0 %
Add: Bentonite	3.0 %

Self-Glazing Clay B

Cone 2-6

Bicarbonate of Soda	4.0 %
Borax	1.0
Dolomite	4.0
Soda Ash	4.0
Whiting	3.0
Cedar Heights Goldart Clay	24.0
Kentucky OM 4 Ball Clay	24.0
Silica (200 mesh)	26.0
No. 1 Silica Sand	10.0
	100.0 %
Add: Bentonite	3.0 %

Color variations of the preceding midrange recipes are possible with the following additions:

Purple/Blue	
Cobalt Carbonate	0.7 %
Turquoise/Green	
Copper Carbonate	2.5-3.0 %
Light Green	
Copper Carbonate	0.5 %
Yellow Green	
Chrome Oxide	1.0-3.0 %
Brown/Purple	
Manganese Dioxide	3-5.0 %
Lemon Yellow	
Vanadium Pentoxide	5-7.5 %
Blue	
Cobalt Oxide	0.25-1.0 %
Tan/Brown	
Iron Oxide	3.0-7.0 %

Egyptian Paste

Cone 08-06

Bicarbonate of Soda	8.3 %
Dolomite	5.1
Soda Ash	4.1
Custer Feldspar	39.2
Kaopaque 20	15.5
Kentucky OM 4 Ball Clay	5.1
Silica (200 mesh)	18.6
No. 1 Silica Sand	4.1
	100.0 %
Add: Bentonite	3.1 %

Colorant additions achieve the following results in heavy reduction or raku:

Copper Luster	
Copper Chloride	0.5-1.0 %
Tin Chloride	0.5-0.75 %
Manganese Dioxide	0.25 %
Yellow/Gold Iridescence	
Iron Chloride	1.0 %
Bismuth Subnitrate	0.5 %
Blue/Silver Iridescence	
Cobalt Chloride	0.25 %
Bismuth Subnitrate	0.5 %
Black Luster	
Cobalt Carbonate	1.0 %
Copper Carbonate	3.0 %
Iron Oxide	5.0 %
Manganese Dioxide	4.0 %

All colors are progressively subdued as temperature increases. Iridescent colors are fugitive at about cone 01.

Homage to Palissy

by John McCuistion

"Hidden Light," 18 inches in diameter, slip-cast low-fire clay; above is a detailed view of the screen print and layered glazes.

Several years ago while visiting the Getty Center in Los Angeles, I had the good fortune to see a ceramic basin attributed to the French artist, Bernard Palissy. I came upon this piece quite by chance, and its beauty and timeless qualities stunned me. Seeing that piece had a profound effect on me. I needed to know more and began to look for any published material on Palissy's work and life.

After reading an excellent book titled Bernard Palissy, written by Leonard N. Amico, I was motivated to further study so I traveled to England and France to see Palissy's work firsthand. This direct observation was critical in understanding how he worked with surface, color and form. On an artistic level, the work of Palissy has much to offer. There is a timeless quality to his work, and I personally believe him to be one of the most important and influential ceramics artists of all time.

How Palissy made his pieces remains a mystery. When he died at about the age of 80, he took many of his artistic secrets with him to the grave. Perhaps maintaining secrecy protected him and his family. During his lifetime, his artwork was sought after and valued by royalty and the ruling elite, but as a Protestant living in a Catholic country he feared for his life. He was imprisoned on three different occasions for his religious beliefs and died in the Bastille.

Scholarly debate continues on how many surviving Palissy pieces are authentic. There is considerable difficulty, and it may be impossible to ever know, what pieces Palissy actually worked on. It was common practice at the time not to sign ceramic works. All of the works on display at the Victoria & Albert Museum, British Museum and the Wallace Collection, for instance, catalog the work in the following manner: "attributed to Palissy and Atelier or close follower."

After studying Palissy's work, I made a radical change in the direction of my artistic work. I became less involved with the form. This

"Trials and Tribulations," 18 inches in diameter, slip-cast low-fire clay, by John McCuistion.

work is about surface, color and recognizable imagery to develop the content. It pays homage to Palissy's rustic ceramics.

The themes in this work deal with air, land, water and the magical natural world around us. Through my work I am able to contribute to the long tradition of the artist as teacher, recorder and seer. The life of an artist is as important and meaningful as any in society.

A Modern Twist on an Old Idea

Here are the steps involved in the process I developed using contemporary materials. I create a slip-cast platter using low-fire clay. After it is thoroughly dry, I wipe the surface with a wet cloth, chamois or sponge. This creates a texture that traps color residues during the washing of the underglaze. It is worth noting that even lightly wiped surfaces can yield dramatic results. Dry the work thoroughly before starting to decorate.

After bisque firing, cover the front side of the platter with one coat of underglaze (usually black). Fill the piece with water and agitate as if panning for gold. The underglaze will settle into the abraded areas and highlight the texture. My choice of underglaze is Duncan Concepts.

The piece is decorated using silk-screen images and allowed to dry. Underglazes are applied over the images—as many as three coats are required per color and I use up to five colors (though there is no limit). Thorough drying is required between each coat of color and the piece must be completely dry prior to washing.

The platter is then completely filled with water, and washed, scraped and wiped to reveal the desired results. After drying, additional color is applied to the surface and the piece is touched up as needed. On the rim and back, I apply three coats of underglaze, allowing time for drying between each coat. Finish with three coats of clear glaze applied to the front and back.

The finished, dried piece is then fired to cone 04 with a 15-minute soak. I allow the kiln to cool for two days before opening.

Kelly King
Surface and Form

by Jennifer Graff

"Nestle, Nuzzle, Run for Cover," 9 inches in height, slab-built cone 10 porcelain, fired to cone 6, china paints.

Kelly King is an artist concerned with fusing unique functional forms with personal content. Her recent covered jars, platters and other vessels serve as familiar utilitarian objects as well as canvases for her innermost ideas. Images of dogs, bundles of birds and sinewy intestines intermingle on the surfaces and ask us to unravel their technical and symbolic mysteries.

King's utilitarian forms are reminiscent of traditional works in clay, yet they achieve a personal and contemporary sense of design. Though the forms initially read as functional pitchers, vases and covered jars, they also easily refer to architectural elements due to their slab construction and vertically stacked components. The forms become metaphors themselves as they gently make reference to the dwellings of the figures and animals that inhabit them. For example, a covered jar can suggest a house for the dogs pictured on the pot while a platter can suggest a nest for a bird. Though often architectural, King's slab work remains fluid as she lets the forms slightly shift where they want to. She is at ease with clay as she allows her building process to be revealed. The pots show seams, slight imperfections and the presence of her hands.

King's carefully crafted slab vessels are made with a creamy white cone 10 porcelain clay body. They are intentionally underfired to cone 6. The clay is not brought to vitrification in order to achieve a stonier clay surface, which provides contrast to

"Dig and Drag," 12 inches in height, slab-built cone 10 porcelain, fired to cone 6, china paints.

the glossy glazes. This process also allows for multiple firings with less danger of cracks forming and prevents the porcelain from warping. Being able to fire repeatedly is important to King because she will often spontaneously draw or add glaze around components of previously fired pieces.

The delicate and calligraphic images of dogs, birds and bones are born out of a love for drawing. King's style of line is confident yet relaxed, as if she were drawing privately in a sketchbook no one would ever see. In addition to linear drawings, King uses the technique of stippling. This employs the use of a small brush that places hundreds of dots in a given space. What is interesting about King's use of the technique is that she creates the positive shapes, or the focal areas, with the absence of dots. These stippled surfaces create an amazing sense of energy.

The drawings of various images are imposed on the surface with a black "ink" made of cobalt-free Mason stain and flux. King uses this on the bare clay surface as well as on a satin white glaze. The black drawings on white clay read like words on a page, and strategic splashes of glossy red, mustard yellow and olive green commercial glazes vibrate on the surface. The glazes, along with the "ink," are fired to cone 6. China paints and gold luster are used in later low-temperature firings for more intense areas of color.

King credits her subconscious for the mix of imagery on her pots. She

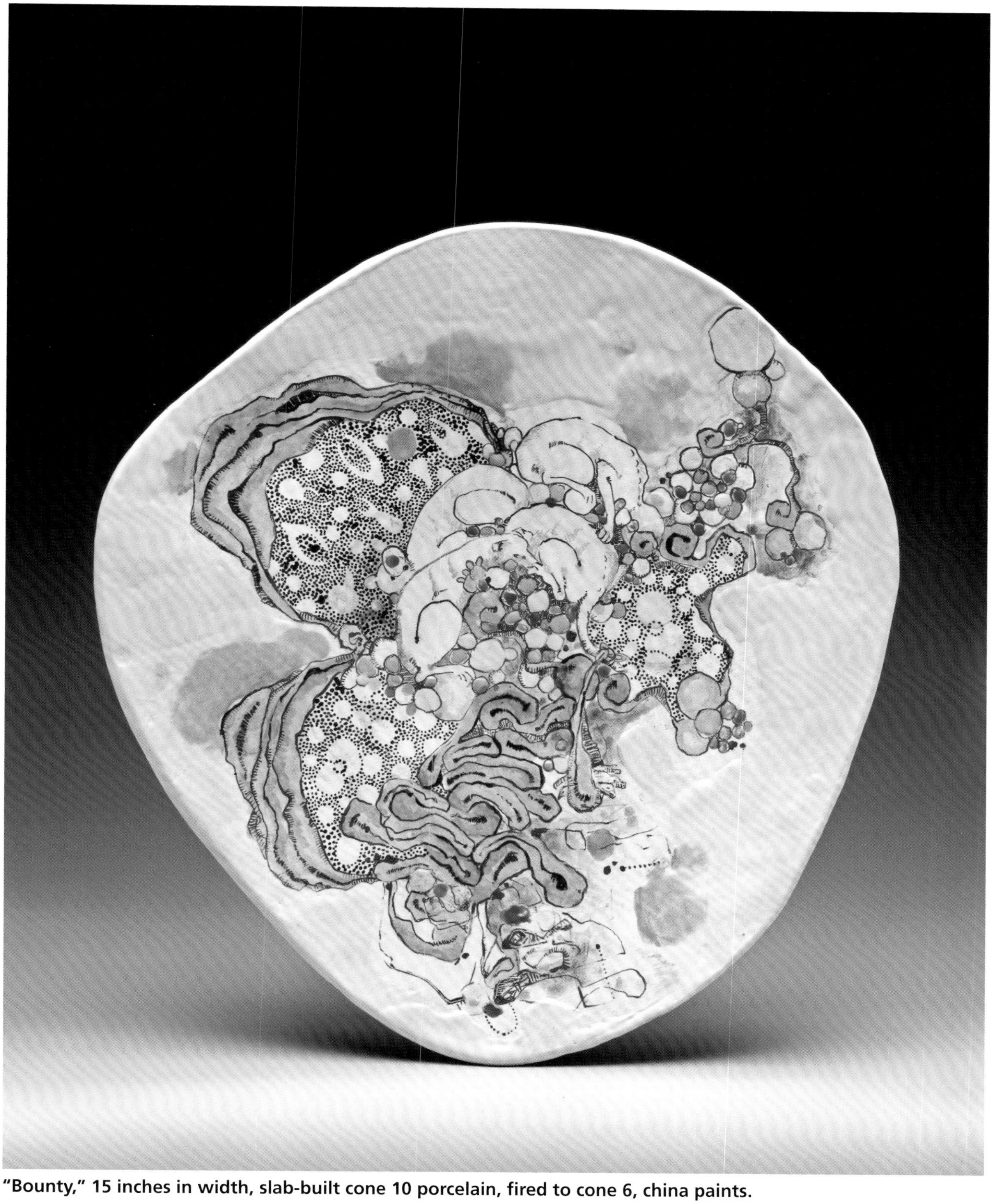

"Bounty," 15 inches in width, slab-built cone 10 porcelain, fired to cone 6, china paints.

is an intuitive artist who has developed the ability to let go and allow what is in her subconscious to come to the surface. She doesn't question where the work is coming from, she just makes it. This uncommon ability allows for a truly personal point of view in her work. Images of dogs, birds, figures, intestines and bones appear because they have real meaning for her; they live in her subconscious. King believes she has come to understand the meaning in the images by processing them long after making them.

Dogs have frequently appeared in King's work throughout the years. She has a deep reverence for dogs and has kept them as pets her entire life. Canines were first used in the work out of a general fascination for their bodies. She was preoccupied with their postures and how this emphasized their joints. Over time, the dogs would transform from mere anatomical studies into wolf-like creatures that symbolized the subconscious. King learned that the presence of dogs insinuates that there is something untamable and inherently wild in all of us.

Birds are another type of animal that grace the surfaces of King's work. They are ever present in many of the pieces although they are often small, obscured and drawn in convoluted clusters. This serves to make them subordinate to other drawings and to appear as decorative elements. Birds have become symbols of beauty and domesticity for King as they have strong associations with the home and childbearing. She is the mother of two small children and describes the presence of birds as representing the archetypal wren; a small nonpredatory songbird that primarily nests and feeds.

The images are not exclusive to dogs and birds and often include domesticated animals and animals raised primarily for consumption. They are all found interacting with the occasional figure, which may only be introduced in the form of a bending arm or the bust of an ambiguous female. However, there are subtle questions raised about the relationship of animals to humans.

The cast of characters curiously pose with images of intestines, repetitions of cell-like forms, and oozing patches of glaze. These almost grotesque elements, juxtaposed against the exquisitely drawn animals, metaphorically speak about King's idea of beauty; that the beauty of a rose could not exist without the rotten compost from which it grows. Presenting both the beautiful and the horrible at once is a quality that King wants in her work. She says in the end, the opposite forces become a metaphor for the self.

King credits all things baroque in influencing the architectural style of the slab-built forms, as well as the decorative nature of the surfaces. In both architecture and painting, the Baroque era was everything dynamic, ornate, theatrical and extravagant. She was greatly affected by once stumbling upon a book of Baroque knives and daggers where

"Birds and Bones," 7 inches in height, slab-built cone 10 porcelain, fired to cone 6, china paints, by Kelly King.

Draw, Paint, Fire, Repeat

by Kelly King

King begins the drawing process on one of her pots. She uses Mason stains, commercial glazes and china paints to create her dynamic surfaces.

I use various techniques that combine painterly surfaces with more tightly rendered images and designs. With each firing, the composition is slowly built upon.

I begin by drawing on leather-hard clay with black mason stain using a fine-tipped brush. I find that drawing on the clay at this stage allows for a more fluid, calligraphic line. After the bisque, a palette of several commercial glazes that combine well with Satin White is applied in layers. These glazes are applied using a flat soft brush for wider coverage and a round bamboo brush to create more of a linear effect and spontaneous drips. I often scrape away exterior layers to reveal areas of pure color before firing the piece to cone 6. The glazing process may be repeated, depending upon the desired effect.

I consider the drips and splatters that occur in both the glazing and firing processes to be an opportunity for further drawing. Using low-fire china paints (Hobby Colorobbia Third Firing Color) and a very small round brush, I apply tiny dots to create both the linear designs and the stippled areas. I initially used this linear stippling technique as a solution to creating a solid line with water-based china paints, which tend to clump and separate. The Third Firing Color "medium" is also helpful in achieving a more uniform consistency with china paints, especially when painting broader areas. Finally, the piece is fired to cone 015.

Recipes

Val Cushing Satin White

Cone 6

Talc	9.0 %
Whiting	16.0
Ferro Frit 3124	9.0
Custer Feldspar	40.0
EPK Kaolin	10.0
Silica	16.0
	100.0%
Add: Bentonite	1.0 %

carvings of animals were woven into the handles of the weapons. King feels motherhood is a strong influence in the work as well, because the pots became more utilitarian and intimate after the arrival of her children.

King initially focused on drawing as a student in the art education program at the University of Georgia in Athens. Being around the likes of Ron Meyers, Michael Simon, Ted Saupe and Andy Nasisse prompted King to take a ceramics course near the end of her program. King would soon complete her art education degree, but as any clay enthusiast would understand, she instantly connected with the material of clay. Her immediate facility with the material gained her acceptance into the University of Georgia's graduate program in ceramics the next year.

King's work is interesting and pertinent contemporary ceramic art. It inspires us to interact with it because it is not oppressively strange, nor is it so ordinarily beautiful that it becomes incidental. We embrace the pots because they are accessible forms. We are challenged by the pots because they carry sophisticated content. The work draws familiar parallels to every human life, and therefore it becomes eternal. The rare gift of this work is that it completes a cycle of creativity between artist and viewer. The artist gives us a unique vision that we bring to life by truly seeing it.

Creating Neriage Blocks

by Faith Rahill

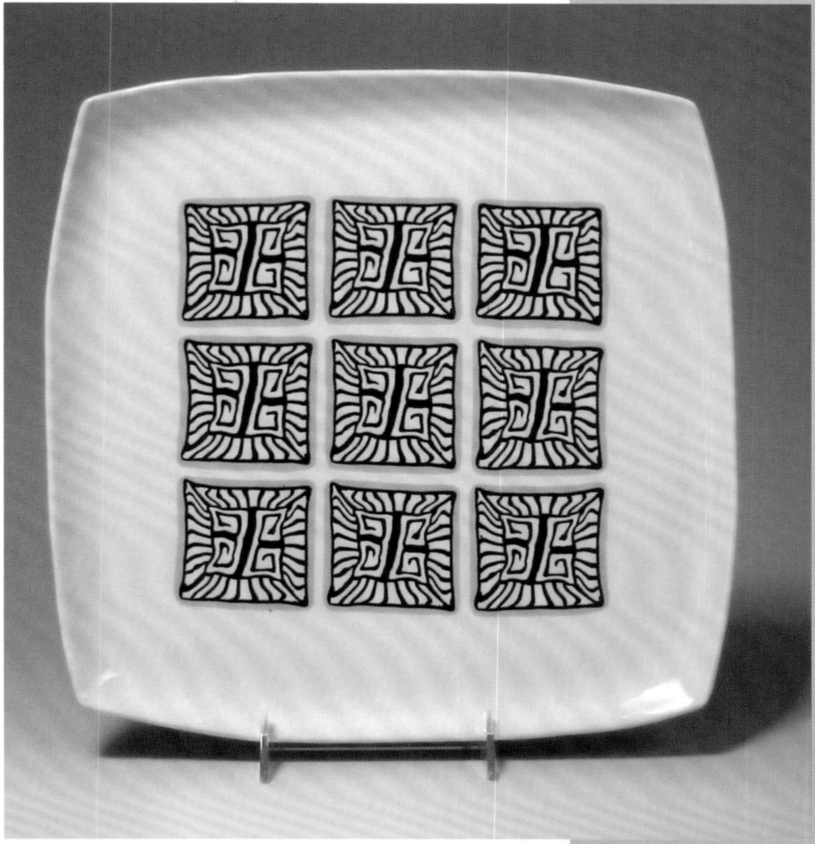

Square plate, 11½ inches in width, white stoneware. From the first time Faith Rahill saw a pot made using the neriage technique as an undergraduate, she has focused exclusively on pursuing and perfecting methods for creating design and pattern using colored clays.

Neriage is a decorative process used in Japan that involves of stacking colored clays then slicing through the cross section to reveal a pattern, which can then be used as an applied decoration. Neriage designs provide a great way to work three dimensionally with patterns and images. The results reflect a combination of careful planning and accidental surprise, plus it's exciting work for those who love patterns and are drawn to the wet-clay stage of pottery making.

My work with colored clays is slow, exacting and fraught with technical challenges. Along with my love of handbuilding, what keeps me hooked on neriage is the pleasure of conceiving a design, followed by the creative challenge of building it in cross section. Slicing through a new block you've been working on for awhile has the same exciting quality of unloading a kiln of new work.

Clay Preparation

Some clays work better than others when it comes to slicing cleanly and not dragging the color. Find white clay you like at any temperature and add your colorants. When working with stacked colored clays, they must be very wet in order for the clay to blend smoothly without seams or cracks. To make the clay wet enough for this technique, add water to new bags of clay and let them sit for a week or more. The uncolored base clay then needs either "sloppy plugging" or to be wedged up with your hands. (My old Bluebird mixer works, but I do have to clean out the de-airing box often.)

Colorants

Measured colorants can be added to any white clay. Since I periodically change my mind about the intensities of color, over time percentages can change. Combining two different colors in a test sometimes yields nice results. Ten percent means, for instance, 5 pounds of wet clay mixed with ½ pound of dry colorant. The colors in this list are Mason stains. You can also use oxides. Years ago I bought 5 and 10 pound batches not knowing that it was a lifetime supply. If you choose to fire at lower temperatures, there are more colors available to you, as some colors burn out at higher temperatures. Here's a list to use as a guideline.

Mason Stains

Black 6600	5.0%
Peacock Blue 6396	7.5%
Lavender 6319	10.0%
Manganese Alumina Pink 6020	10.0%*
Avocado 6280	9.0%*
Titanium Yellow 6485	10.0%
Mazerine Blue 6300	1–3.0%

* or less

Blending

To add color, create a well in a preweighed lump of wet clay and spoon the weighed dry material into the well. Add just enough water to make a paste, then slowly mix it together until well blended and wedged. There are hand cream products that can help protect your skin while wedging colors into clay. I recommend buying one and applying it before getting to work. I use Kerodex®, which comes from the pharmacist.

Two different clays, such as a brown and a white stoneware, can be used together if they shrink compatibly. With all the colorants and clays available, experimentation is a great way to discover what you like and to create your own colors.

Making a Block

For this neriage design, slice thin slabs of uncolored and black-colored clay blocks using 4 lb. fishing line. Roll the slabs together from both ends to form a double spiral (figure 1). Work on plastic or a wet canvas surface to keep everything as wet as possible. To create the center of the block, press two of the double spirals together back to back (figure 2).

To create the stripes, stack thin, alternating black and white slabs together (figure 3). Use 2 lb. fishing line to cut the block in half (figure 4). Cut each half again to create four sections. Since the fishing line is hard to see, tie one end of the line to a button so that it's easier to find when you need it.

Slam the double-spiral square on the table to make it flat on all sides, then place the stripe blocks against it (figure 5). Squish the block into a square, forcing the corners to meet, then slam the block again to make it a square (figure 6).

Wrap a thin slice of green-colored clay around the block to give it a border (figure 7), then gently slam it once more to create a good bond. Place the block on a clean, wet can-

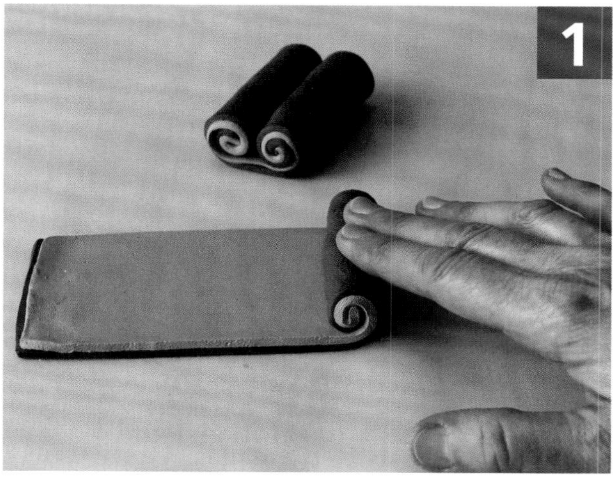

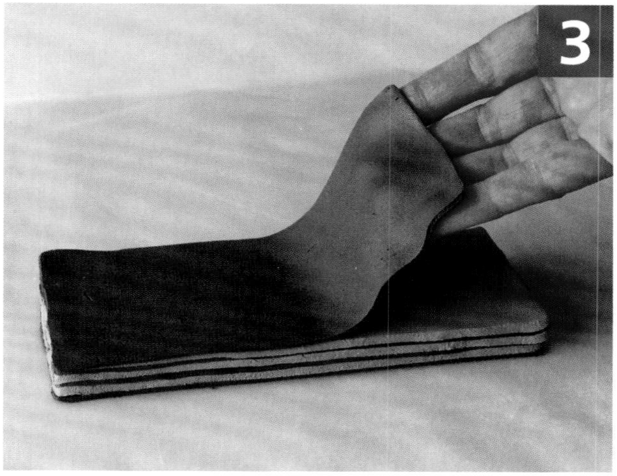

vas surface and slice it with 2 lb. fishing line across the bottom. Use mat-board slats as guides (figure 8).

Carefully peel the slice off of the block (figure 9). Slice all the pieces you're going to need for the next day, and store them between wet handi-wipes or wet pieces of cloth under plastic. The slices need to be soggy all the way through in order for them

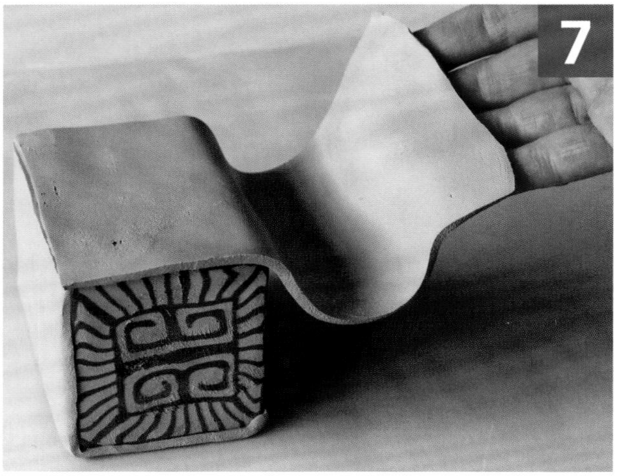

to roll seamlessly into a slab of clay.

Arrange the slices on a rolled out slab that is sitting on plastic (figure 10). To keep the clay from sticking to the rolling pin, use a piece of cloth between the pin and the clay (figure 11). Slats keep the rolling even. You'll see a print of the design when you remove the cloth. Note: An important part of my routine consists of washing my cloths out at the end of the day and draping them across my studio.

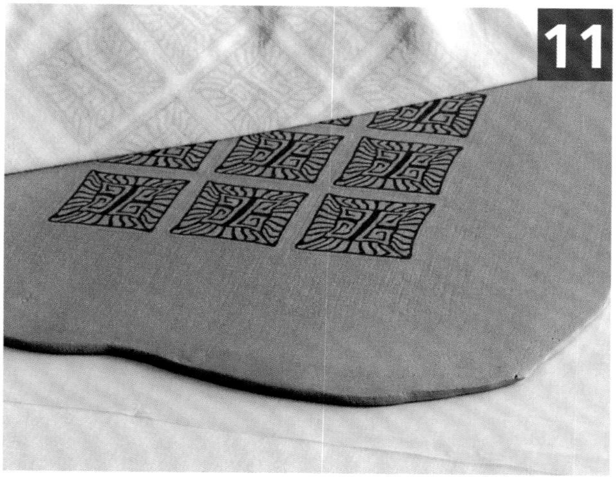

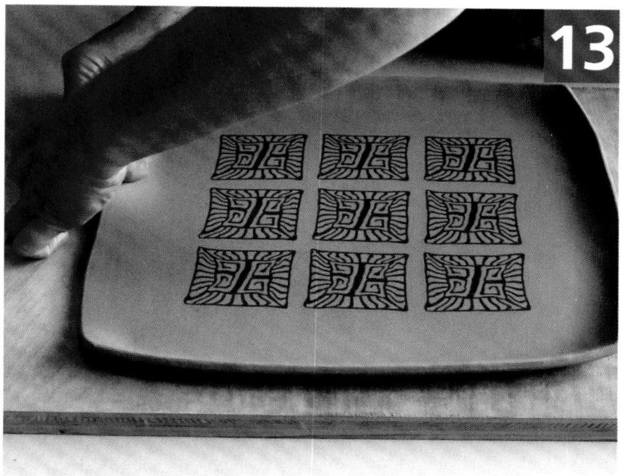

Once the surface of the slab seems dry enough that the rolling pin won't drag the color around, roll without the cloth (figure 12). Wipe the rolling pin off after each pass, otherwise you might have to sand at the bisque stage to clean up stray colored clay. Use a cardboard template to cut the final shape of the plate. After lifting the edge to form the sides (figure 13), I always cover the piece and allow it to dry slowly on a bat (until there's lots of lovely black mold under it). Slow drying reduces warping and allows the moisture to equalize among all the combined clays so they dry uniformly.

Rectangular plate, 9¼ inches in length. The creative challenge of building a design in cross section in a block keeps Rahill hooked on this process.

Chicken plate, 8¼ inches in diameter. This plate shows how several patterns can be successfully incorporated into a single piece.

Laura Kukkee
Slip Decoration

by Anderson Turner

Untitled, 23 inches in diameter, monoprinted (paint, slip trail, silk screen) slips on soft slabs, glazes and sand then multifired.

It is often taught that artists must strive to be wholly original. We must envision something great and new and then apply it to our art, thus astounding all who happen by the work we've made. This is a tall order to say the least. Many a great idea has fallen by the way side because the artist is unsure of how to execute the desired result. Often, it is the subtle change in a technique that can lead to impressive results. One example of that type of change is in the work of artist Laura Kukkee.

Laura a native of Toronto, Canada did her undergraduate studies with Bruce Cochrane at The Sheridan School of Crafts and Design in Oakville, Ontario and developed this technique in the craft studios at Harbour Front Centre in Toronto. Utilizing slip or engobe in the decoration of clay has been happening for thousands of years. From the Ancient Greeks and Chinese to the 17th century country English potter, the use of colored slip has been an important part of the decorative arsenal of nearly every clay artist.

Laura is currently working with ideas surrounding the notion of a fragment. "This fragment is in the form of an image or a pattern which is divorced from its original meaning. By pulling fragments outside of their traditional contexts and

Slip Trailing Appliqué

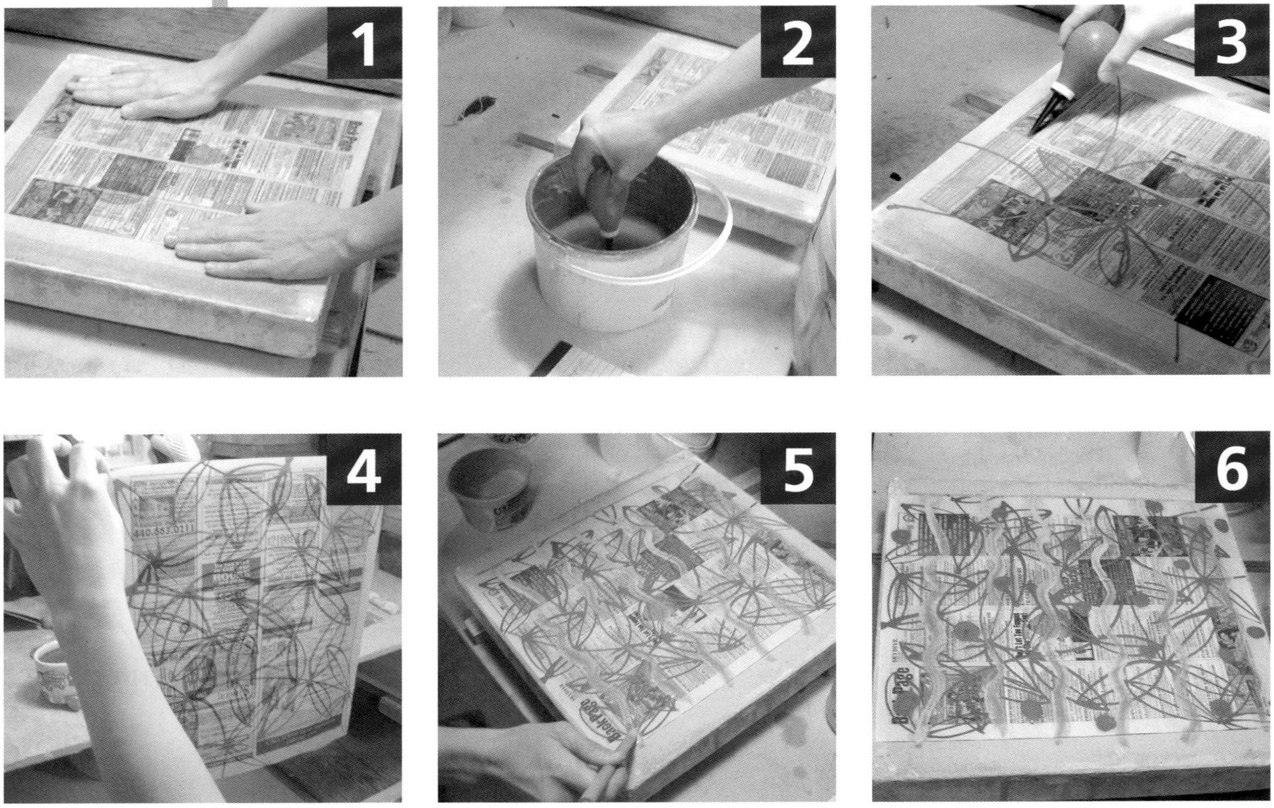

restructuring the way in which they are presented, meanings become more elastic." Her results in the research are both exciting and new, and they offer a chance for individuality that every artist strives for.

Notes on Slip

Slip, as defined by Vince Pitelka in his book *Clay: A Studio Handbook*, is clay suspended in water, usually the consistency of thick cream. It may be colored and used to decorate surfaces, or may be cast into plaster molds to create ceramic forms. For her artwork, Laura uses slip the consistency of a thick cream as well as slip that is substantially thinner. She uses different proportions of water and a small amount of Darvan #7 to get the "flow" of the slip she desires. It's a good idea to test all slips, engobes and glazes before using them on your own work.

Slip Trailed Appliqué

What you'll need: ball syringe, newsprint, spray bottle and plaster slab (optional). Laura sets the plaster on two pieces of wood to keep slab well ventilated, thus discouraging mold. You will also need the colored slips of your choice.

Wet a piece of newsprint using a spray bottle so that it is damp but not soaked. Smooth the paper out

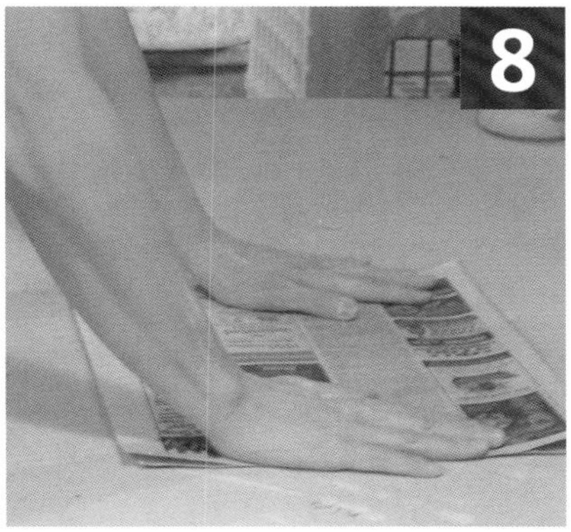

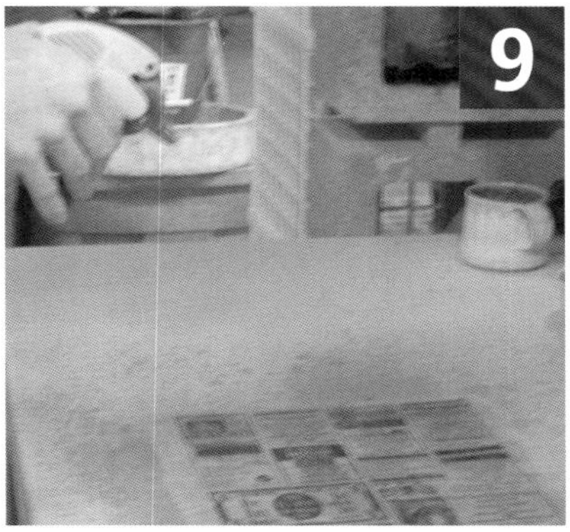

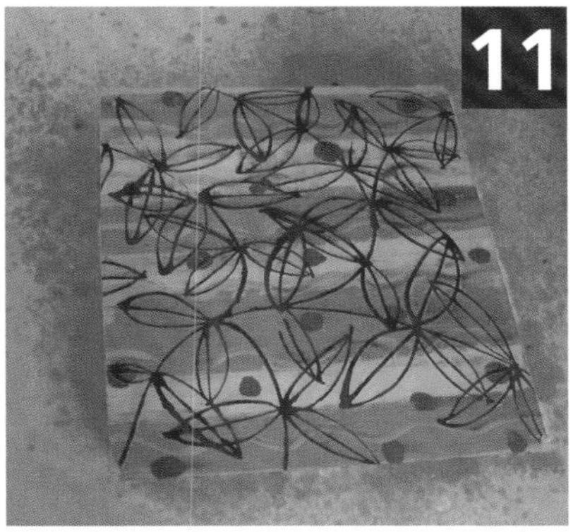

onto the plaster slab, so you don't get ridges—smoothing helps the paper absorb water (figure 1).

Remember, whatever color you use first is going to be the outline of the pattern you're making. You're building color and pattern from the top layer down with the background color applied last, which is the opposite direction one normally works. For this demo I'm using black slip, though I have often used other colors. It's a good idea to mix and sieve slip thoroughly beforehand to blend all the materials.

Dip the syringe in the slip and fill it (figure 2). To get the bulb flowing, try practicing on an extra sheet of paper before beginning (figure 3). Slip trail pattern or image of your choice onto paper. Pick the paper up by the edges carefully and hold it up to light so you can see your pattern better (figure 4). Set the paper aside and allow slip to dry until the shine goes away, then start laying color in and around the pattern (figure 5).

I like to apply bands of color together behind the pattern. Set aside the paper and let dry until gloss disappears (figure 6).

Again, once gloss is gone, cover the colored slip with a white slip made of the same ingredients as your clay body, with roughly 3% Darvan #7 added to the mixture. Make sure the

TIP

I store clay slabs I've already made by wrapping them in plastic. I usually have 20 of these sheets going at one time, so I can work with them like I'm making a collage or quilt.

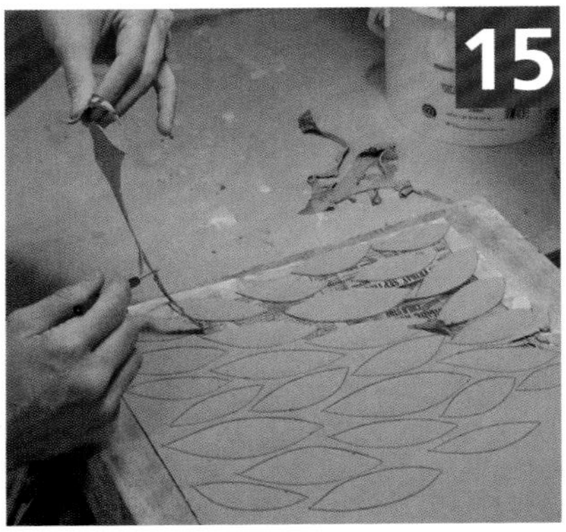

Recipes

Sheridan Studio Colored Slip

Cone 6-10

Grolleg Kaolin	45.8%
Kona F4 Feldspar	24.6
Pyrophyllite	8.2
Bentonite	5.1
Silica	16.3
	100.0%

Plus 15% stain of your choice.

Clay Body

Cone 6

6 Tile Clay	50 lb
EPK Kaolin	25
Kentucky OM4 Ball Clay	25
G200 Feldspar	45
Ferro Frit 3124	10
Silica	45
Whiting	4
Bentonite*	3

Plus 2 handfuls of Epsom salts

* soak bentonite overnight.

slip is really flowing. Set aside and allow to dry until the gloss goes away or you're ready to use. I often make up to four applications of white slip depending on how thick I want the slab to be. Usually though, one application is enough (figure 7).

Take the slip-trailed sheet and cover with paper, then smooth (figure 8). Flip the slab over, keeping the new sheet of paper in place. Spray the paper with water until damp. Flatten the paper so that water spreads evenly (figure 9). Begin peeling the corner of the paper, being careful not to rip the clay sheet (figure 10). This will reveal the slip-trailed pattern (figure 11).

Take another piece of paper and place it over the pattern. Make sure to smooth it out, as this helps remove moisture (figure 12). Flip the slab over and remove the paper (figure 13). Now you're ready to cut shapes to apply to your pot, based upon your design (figure 14).

Remove excess clay from around the shapes (figure 15). Gently peel up one of your shapes. Brush slip onto the white side of the piece using the same white slip. Because of the Darvan #7, there is no need to score (figure 16). Gently press the piece onto the pot or sculpture you've made. The pot should be soft leather hard (figure 17).

Inlaying Slip Appliqué

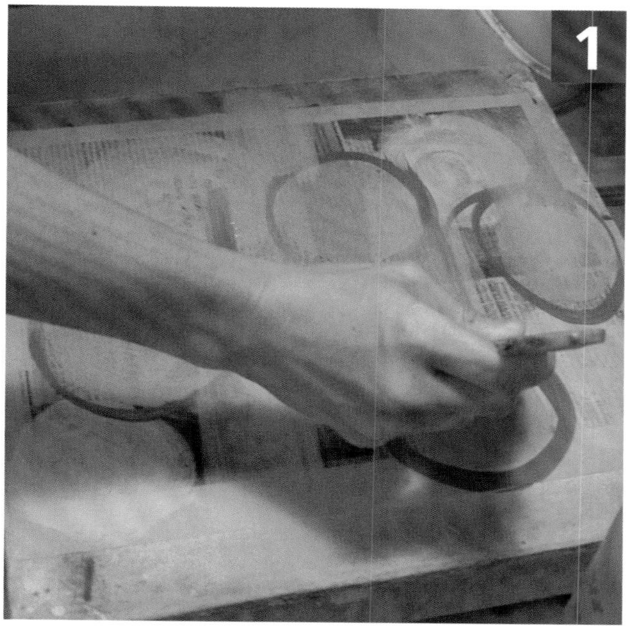

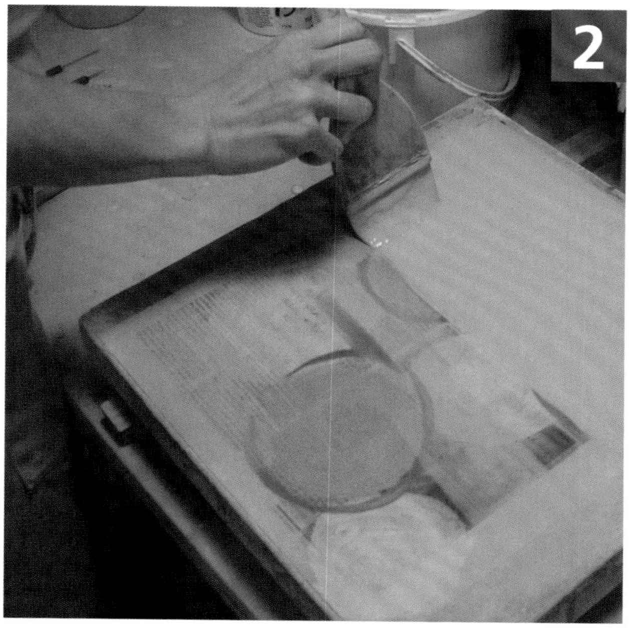

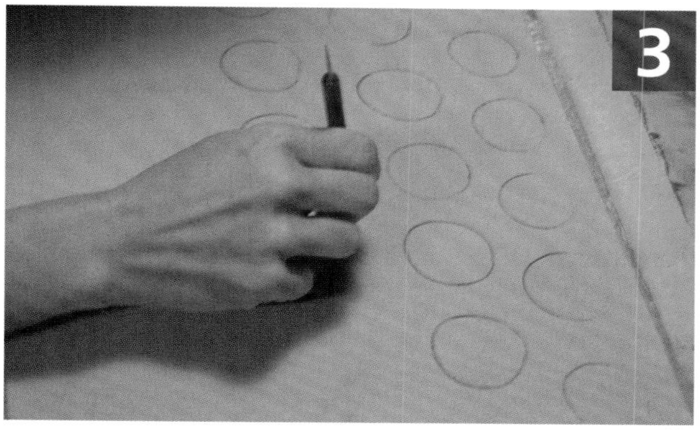

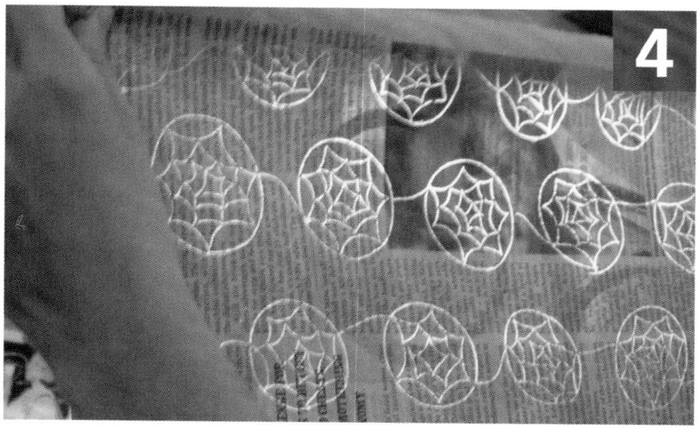

Inlaying Slip Appliqué

Begin this process in exactly the same way as the slip trailing. Brush the slips in a design covering the paper. In this example Rahill is using a large pattern and bold colors. Set the paper aside to dry (figure 1).

Once the gloss is gone, cover the design with the white slip made from your clay body with approximately 3% Darvan #7 added to the mixture. Set aside (figure 2).

When the gloss has dissappeared from the white slip, carve shapes in the slip. Be careful not to cut through the newspaper (figure 3).

When you finish the pattern you should be able to see light through the design. Cover entire sheet with black slip. Set aside to dry. When the gloss is gone, cover entire piece with white slip (figure 4).

Smooth a sheet of newspaper over the slab, flip it over and carefully

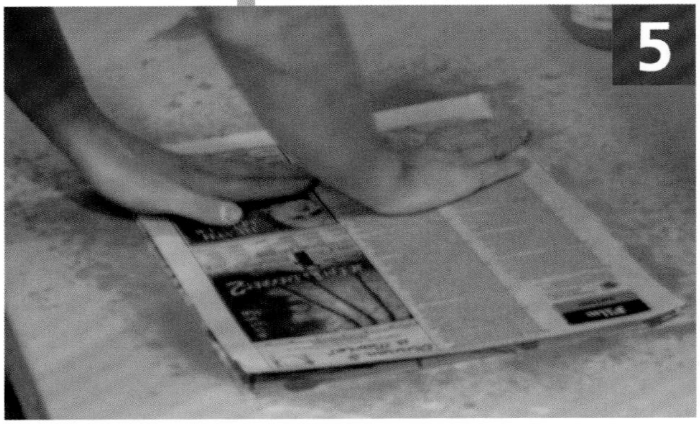
5

6

7

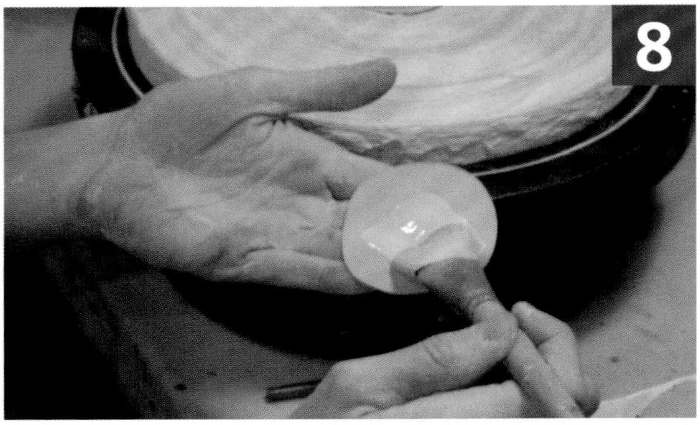
8

remove the paper from the pattern side, and spray with water, if necessary, to keep from tearing the slab (figure 5).

Place fresh paper over the slab, smooth and flip the slab again. Peel the paper off the back of the slab. The slab can now be cut into shapes for appliqué (figure 6).

Once the excess clay is removed from between the shapes, begin to gently peel up the cut out patterns (figure 7).

Paint white slip onto the white side of each piece and gently apply the shape to the pot (figure 8).

Silk-Screening Slip Appliqué

Silk Screening Appliqué

Items you need: squeegee, spatula, metal rib, small pitcher, brushes, a pointed tool and various colored slips. Prepare paper the same way as in the previous examples (figure 1). Position the silk screen on top of the prepared paper (figure 2). Pour a bead of black slip on the screen at one end only (figure 3). Squeegee slip across the screen with steady, even pressure (figure 4). Use a metal rib to remove excess slip from the silk screen (figure 5). Carefully remove the paper from the silk screen to avoid tearing the pattern (figure 6).

After the pattern is screened onto the paper, let it dry until the gloss is gone (figure 7). Apply colored slip over the design and allow to dry (figure 8). After the slip loses its gloss, cover the entire sheet with white slip and set aside to dry (figure 9). Flip and add fresh newspaper. When this process is completed, begin to cut out the shapes (figure 10) Once the excess clay is removed, gently peel up the cut out shapes (figure 11). Paint white slip onto the white side of the shape and apply it to the pot (figure 12).

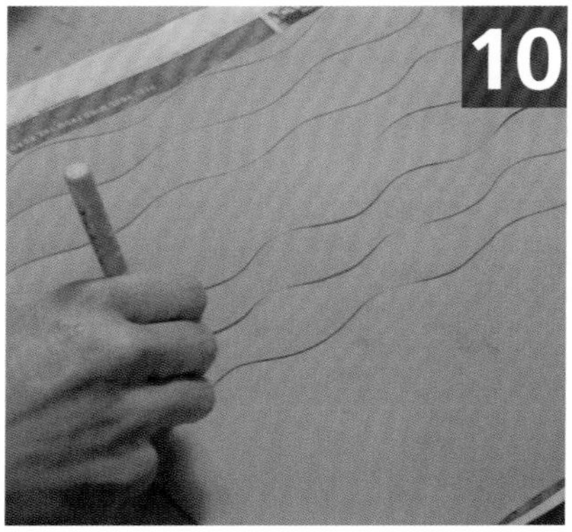

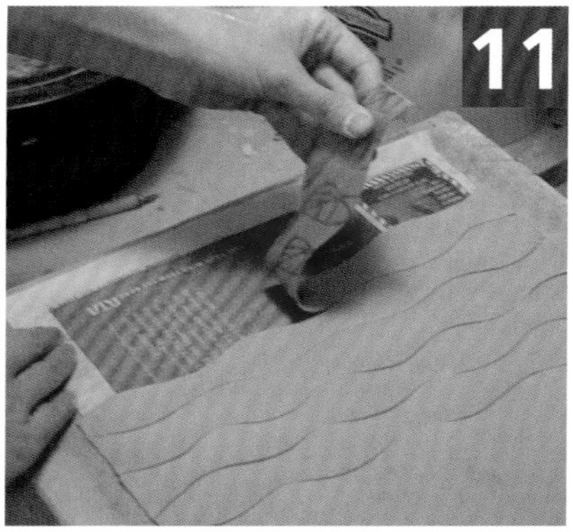

Three completed forms with applied slip decoration.

Testing Your Clay

by Paul Andrew Wandless

The more you know about the materials you use the better off you'll be. These tests are valuable in revealing general qualities about a clay body at different temperatures. This kind of information goes a long way in helping you decide if a clay body is really matching your needs in the studio.

At some point we all change clay bodies for one reason or another. Whether you want a body that shrinks less, has more absorption/less absorption, a lower/higher maturation point or just a different color, there are hundreds of commercial clays to choose from. While most clays have pretty good general catalog descriptions of what they are and what they can do, once we apply our specific working and firing processes, other issues can arise. A combination of tests can give you plenty of information that makes choosing and learning about a clay body a little easier.

Why Test?

Testing clay bodies provides you with information that you can observe, touch and feel first hand in your own environment. While a catalog photo shows what a clay may look like fired at one or several cones, it may not tell you what it will do at the cone you're firing to. Basic clay bar tests give you information more specific to your needs, and a 25-pound sample is usually enough to complete all the tests you need.

What to Test

Tests should be done at multiple temperatures to yield the widest range of information on the clay body. You need to understand the same general characteristics at every temperature you fire to, and even at temperatures you may want to fire to in the future. I test at every potential cone I may fire to and keep records of all the results.

The three important general characteristics to take note of are

Prepare test trays from high fire clay.

Prepare triangular stilts to support bar.

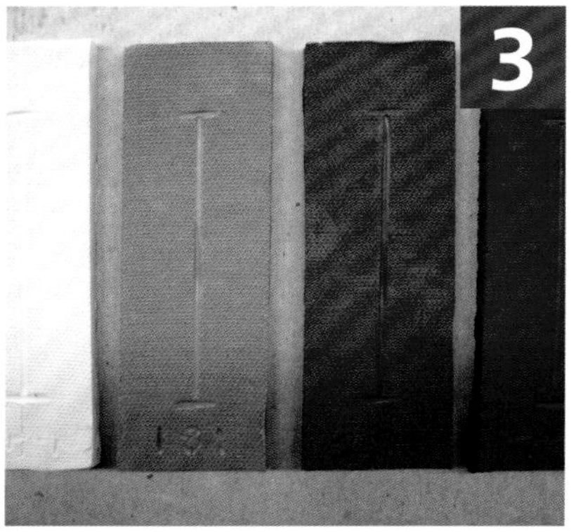

Four test bars with 10 cm. line.

shrinkage, absorption and warping/slumping. Other important qualities to note are color, texture, plasticity and hardness. Some results are determined with visual and touch tests while others require simple formulas. All require consistency of procedure so the results you achieve are created under the same conditions.

Firing Box and Stilts

When firing above a recommended temperature—either on purpose or by mistake—clay bodies start to melt and fuse or stick to the shelves. To test clay bars, you'll need a shallow firing box to protect your kiln shelves and to make handling and transportation easier. You'll also need clay stilts for the warping test.

Using a high-fire clay, make a simple clay box that's 8–10 inches square with a 1-inch wall. Make several boxes at the same time so you can test multiple bodies in the same firings or just have them on hand for future use (figure 1).

Make triangle stilts about the thickness of your pinky and long enough to span the width of the clay bar (figure 2). All stilts must be the same height.

Clay Bars

You'll need three clay bars for each body you're testing. For consistency and accuracy of results, use the same dimensions for all your clay bars. While some tests yield correct results regardless of the bar dimensions, you can always rule out size and dimension as variables that could cause any irregularities. I make ¼-inch-thick bars measuring 2 inches wide by 6 inches long. If your work is thicker, make bars to match, but don't exceed ½ inches in thickness. After cutting the bars to size, draw a 10-cm-long line on one of them with a hash mark at each end. This will be used for a shrinkage test later (figure 3).

For the tests here, I've selected four bodies to test: two white bodies from Standard (#257 Grolleg Porcelain Cone 8–10 and #181 White Stoneware Cone 6–10) and two from Amaco (#29 Brown Stone Earth-

Dry trays and bars slowly and evenly.

Place one bar on stilts and two of them flat in the tray.

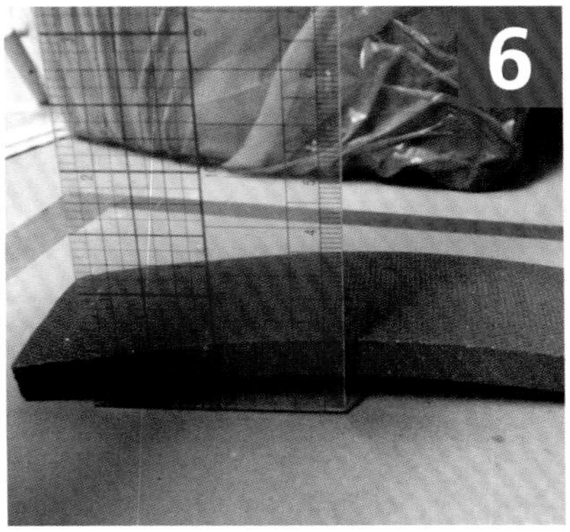

After each firing, measure the amount of deflection.

enware Cone 06–04 and #77 Terra Cotta Clay Cone 5). All four bodies have different characteristics at the temperatures to which I'm interested in firing them, and testing several bodies at the same time takes better advantage of each firing. Remember to write the clay number on the back of each tile.

Once all bars are cut and firing boxes are built, let them dry to bone dry. They can be stacked with newspaper layered in between and a board on top for a little weight to keep them from warping. It's important that the firing boxes and clay bars stay flat while drying to assure accurate test results (figure 4).

Before the Bisque

At the bone dry stage, visually examine the bars for a color change if any. Use a ruler to measure in centimeters the shrinkage line to see if it has changed from its original 10 cm length. Record the results.

For each firing, place the bars side by side in the firing box, and place one of them on the triangle stilts. The stilts should be placed about ¼- to ½-inch in from the ends of the bar. If the stilts are too close, the bar may not warp or slump to its fullest potential. The shrinkage bar and the other regular bar are simply placed in the bottom of the box.

Firing

While the test firing can be done in any kiln, the results are most applicable if done in the same kiln used for your work. Indicate in your notebook or worksheet if it's an electric or gas kiln, oxidation or reduction firing, salt, wood, soda, etc. For best results, start firings at the lowest cone temperature and then progressively refire the bars at higher cones until the highest desired cone is reached. A sample for progressive test firings for a cone 10 clay body would be cone 06, cone 01, cone 6 then finally cone 10.

Clay Bar Tests

The following traditional tests give a good range of basic information that helps you to better understand your clay body. Keep good records in your

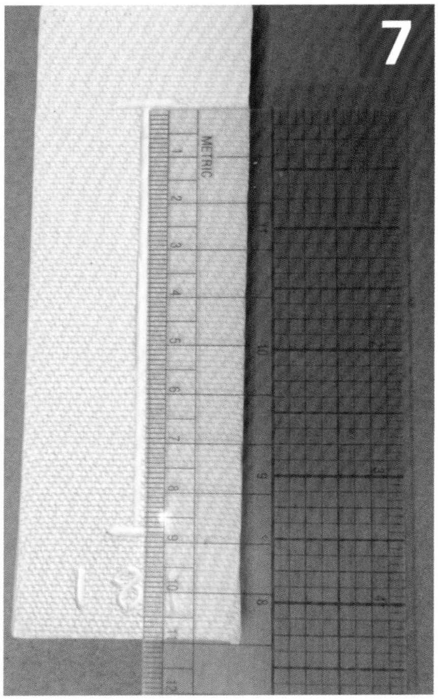

Measure the 10 cm line to determine shrinkage.

notebook so you'll have the results for future reference. If there are other specific qualities, such as glaze fit or color effect, test for these also.

Warping/Slumping

Visually examine for any warping or sagging movement in the center. Remove the bar from the stilts, turn it over and place it on a flat surface so the gap (if any) can be measured (figure 6). This test informs you at what temperature the walls may start to warp or deform or a plate may begin to slump. The information can be applied to the sculptural or structural applications of the clay body. An exact percentage for this is not as important as just knowing when the clay body starts to move.

Soak bars in water and weigh them after 24 hours.

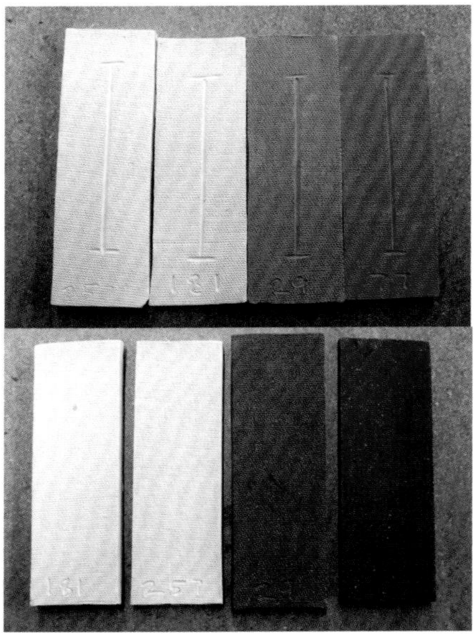

Note the color of the clay after each firing. Here are four clays fired to cone 04 (top) and cone 7 (bottom).

Shrinkage Test

Measure the length of the line in centimeters on the shrinkage bar (figure 7), and subtract it from 10 (based on the original 10 cm line). For example, 10 cm – 8.5 cm = 1.5 cm. An easy way to convert this result to a percentage is to move the decimal to the right one place, so 1.5 cm means 15% shrinkage. Knowing the shrinkage rate helps in determining which glazes will fit the body and even which two bodies can be used together.

Absorption Test

There are two types of tests that can determine the absorption of a clay body. One is a simple visual test and the other is a weight calculation. For the visual test, place a few drops of a liquid (like ink) on the surface of the bar to create a stain. Let it soak in for an hour then wash off the surface with water. The darker the stain, the more absorbent the clay. This is not an exact test, but it gives a quick and useful general result.

The weight calculation test is more specific. Weigh the fired bar on a gram scale and record the result (figure 8). Soak the bar in water for 24 hours, pat dry, then weigh again and record the result. Subtract the first weight (dry bar) from the second weight (water soaked bar) to get the weight of the absorbed water. Divide the weight of the absorbed water by the original dry weight and move the decimal two places to the right to find the absorption rate.

Example: Original bar weight of 4.2 grams is subtracted from soaked bar weight of 4.6 grams giving you an absorbed water weight of .4 grams. Divide .4 by 4.2 which equals .095 making absorption 9.5%.

Color Test

Visually examine a bar to see if there has been a color change (figure 9). The color change can sometimes be dramatic depending on the cone it was fired and is important for aesthetic purposes. It can also help you determine the best glazes to work visually on the surface.

Surface/Texture

Visually examine the bar to determine if the surface has changed. Run your fingers across the bar to see if it's the same, smoother or coarser. This information is important aesthetically and helps you determine if it meets your visual and tactile needs.

Hardness

Using a nail, see if you can scratch the surface to see how hard or soft it is at the fired temperature. This test helps determine the surface durability at different temperatures.

Building a Gas/Electric Kiln

by Mel Jacobson

Finished Pieces: Nice reds, Shinos, and good body color achieved in firing.

To get a reducing atmosphere in an electric kiln, one must add some type of reducing agent, such as gas. Normally, electric kilns are fired in a neutral or oxidizing atmosphere, and the elements develop a somewhat protective coating of oxidized alumina. During reduction, this coating reverts to the metal and the elements can get smaller, and layers of the element can even spall. While elements can be reoxidized in subsequent firings, both their efficiency and life expectancy are greatly reduced.

To preserve metal elements, they need to be protected from the kiln atmosphere, and ITC (International Technical Ceramics, Inc.) produces a nonconductive coating that does just that. In the following photos, Mel leads a hands-on demonstration that followed the Nils Lou method for creating one of these small gas/electric hybrid kilns.

Take an electric kiln completely apart, and remove all elements, wires and switches. Drill a 1¼-inch hole in the center of the top and bottom (figure 1). Thoroughly clean the kiln. While a vacuum cleaner works, using compressed air does a great job, but because of the dust, work outside and wear a mask (figure 2). New elements have a thin manufacturing film on them so clean them well in household bleach using a small brush. Rinse them well and hang to dry (figure 3). Mix 3 parts of ITC 213 with 1 part water in a blender. Estimate what you need, and make more if necessary or store excess in an airtight container (figure 4). Thoroughly coat the coils by dipping them. Use a sheet-rock mud pan or a 5-gallon bucket. Hang the coils up to dry (figure 5). Lightly spray the inside of the kiln with water. This allows the ITC to form a more even coating (figure 6). Add 2 parts of ITC 100 to 1 part water and mix thoroughly with a power mixer. The ITC settles fast so you will have to keep agitating (stirring the bucket) as you work. It helps to have two people (figure 7). Using 90 lbs. of pressure in the air compressor and a sandblaster/spray gun, spray the kiln with an even coat of about 1/32 to 1/16 inch thick (figure 8). After the ITC dries, install the coils; use original instructions that came with the kiln (figure 9). Reinstall and check all Kiln Sitter parts. Reconnect all wires after you make sure all fittings are tight and clean and the connections have been sandpapered. Note the overspray that came out of the peep holes. This does no harm, but you can clean it off if you wish (figure 10). Now spray the entire interior—coils and all—with a second coat of ITC 100. Make sure it is all well covered (figure 11). Buy a nice high-heat Bunsen burner (propane). We used one from Frey Scientific (figure 12). Connect the hose to a 25-pound propane cylinder with a regulator. Fittings are available from gas suppliers (figure 13). Load the kiln. To enhance air flow, and to promote even reduction, use half shelves and stagger them. Full shelves will simply divert the flame to the outside edge of the kiln (figure 14).

MATERIALS

- Kiln—new or good used one (Note: If your kiln is under warranty, this procedure may void it. Contact the manufacturer to check the details for your kiln)
- New electric elements (we ordered ours from Euclids)
- Bleach (household)
- ITC 213 Ceramic Coating for Metals
- ITC 100 Ceramic Coating
- ITC 296A Ceramic Top Coating
- Bunsen burner (Frey Scientific)
- Propane hose and fittings
- 25 lb. Propane cylinder (like the kind used for a barbecue)

SUPPLIES

- 5-gallon bucket
- Glaze mixer
- Blender
- 1¼-inch hole saw/drill bit
- Compressor capable of 90 psi
- Sandblasting gun and hose

SOURCES

Refractory Coating
ITC
(International Technical Ceramics, Inc.)
Available at www.axner.com.

Elements
Euclid Elements
(The Pottery Supply House)
www.euclids.com.

Bunsen Burner
Frey Scientific
www.freyscientific.com

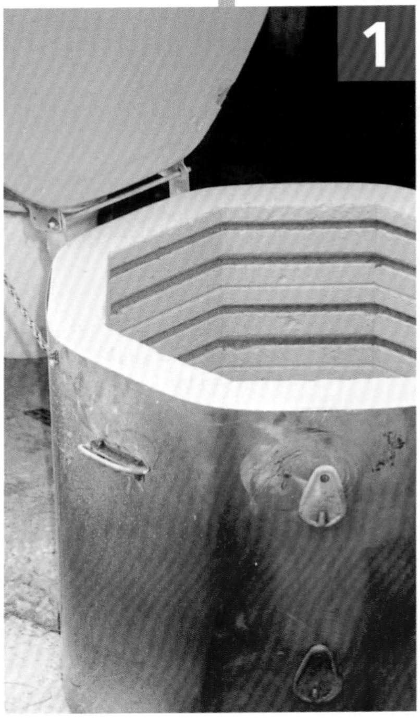
1

2

3

4
Osterizer
cycle blend
ITC 213

5

6

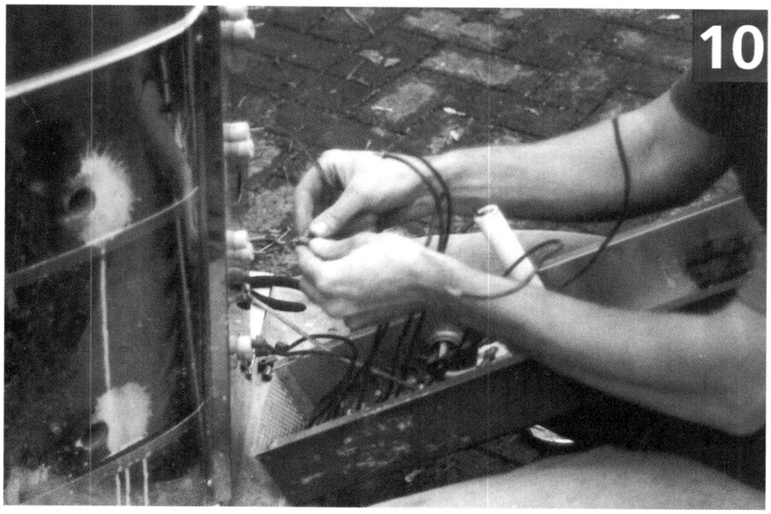

CAUTION

To avoid having the reducing atmosphere leaking out of the kiln and harming electrical components, make sure you plug (with ITC) the holes where your element wires go to the outside of the kiln. Allow the kiln to dry then fire it to cone 08 or so.

OPTIONAL

To obtain a higher degree of purity when firing porcelain, jewelry and other fine items, spray the entire kiln with a coat of ITC 296A Top Coat. To 2 parts of ITC 296A, add 1 part water and mix well. Note: ITC 296A is applied AFTER ITC 100 has been applied and fired.

FIRING INSTRUCTIONS

1. Fire with electricity only until you reach 1750°F.
2. Leaving the electricity on, turn on the gas, light and place Bunsen burner under kiln so that the flame goes up the hole in the bottom.
3. Adjust the reducing atmosphere by partially covering the hole in the lid with a piece of kiln shelf. Move it until you get an inch or more flame from the spy hole on the side of the kiln.
4. Fire until KilnSitter trips and/or witness cones fall.
5. Turn off the gas and electricity. Plug holes in top and bottom of kiln with Kaowool plugs.
6. Optional: If firing a lot of copper reds, soak the kiln (when the kiln cools to 1750°F) by turning the gas back on for about an hour.
7. Allow kiln to cool completely (well, 250°F anyway) before opening.

WARNING: This kiln must be well ventilated!

TIPS

1. Never coat old elements with ITC. It will not work. Always buy new elements.
2. Use a decent used kiln, not a beater. You want a clean, tight soft brick surface to coat with ITC.
3. If the lid doesn't fit tight, make a gasket from thin sheets of Kaowool.
4. Place a piece of Kaowool over the hose under the kiln so it won't be affected by the heat.
5. Kiln shelves may also be coated with ITC 100 to improve resistance to deflection (see photo below).

An Anagama and an Electric Kiln

by Daryn Lowman

Lowman likes to use organic qualities in conjunction with hard lines, or linear architecture, as shown in this stoneware platter, which is 17 inches square. The piece was initially wood fired, then low-fire glazes were brushed on, and it was refired in an electric kiln.

Wood-fired ceramics has gained momentum in the United States, where the ceramics department at any given college or university not only boasts about the quality of its facilities in terms of the number of electric kilns or the size of car kiln, but also the representative atmospheric kiln. The emergence of outdoor kilns—whether they are wood, salt or soda—in ceramics programs is continuing and these processes maintain an evolutionary course.

It has been years since my introduction to kiln construction at the University of Alaska Fairbanks (UAF). The ceramics department there was an energizing place. People gathered there because pots are social; they gathered because it was cold; but mostly they gathered because it was fun to make pots.

As happens when most individuals become entranced with the processes of making ceramics, wood firing has a way of taking over all your time. In graduate school this commitment

Teapot, 9 inches in height, stoneware, with low-fire glazes, wood fired, by Daryn Lowman.

to a specific process can be absorbed, but in life, time is gobbled up by so many tasks. Spending months stacking wood, making work, loading and firing kilns puts a lot of pressure on the work produced.

When considering the quality of wood firing, what is the standard that establishes success? For me a successful wood-fired pot emits a certain energy. It may be the effect of ferocious flames, heat and labor on the surface of a simple coffee cup, or the interior of a platter. However, there are pieces that this labor-intensive process creates that have qualities that are not desirable including unmelted ash, uneven temperatures within the kiln and ineffective flame patterns. That's wood firing for you.

Sometimes pieces that don't appear successful at first can become the "desirables" upon later encounters. Most often, however, the work that simply does not make the cut will sit around and maybe find its way back into the tumultuous environment of flame and ash for another go around.

When I found it difficult to let go of the "undesirable" or wait for the next kiln load, I inadvertently began considering the idea of continuing the process, but this time without flame and with a different application.

While in graduate school at the University of Minnesota, I became increasingly interested in mid-century design and also the work of English painter Ben Nicholson. His colors were straight out of the bucket, the lines crisp and clean, but also, the surface—referencing weathering, touch and time—was intriguing. The surfaces drew me back to rural architecture and the aging qualities of wood and paint; surfaces that contained stories. In the evolution of developing form in my work, I looked toward Korean Yi and Shilla Dynasty wares, American folk pottery, and to landscapes of rural Minnesota.

Integrating these values of process into my own work created many prototypes and discoveries. Initially using soda/salt kilns to play with the mixture of temperatures and to create the first melted layer of information, I quickly found that the glassy uniformity on these surfaces did not develop the desired tensions in textures.

In formulating my work habits, I used the soft, organic qualities of clay, slip and glazes along with crisp, hard lines drawn into the surface. In a sense, I began wrapping the pots with a linear architecture, and utilizing iconographic drawings and shapes to break up the surface.

Within the commitment to any idea or vision there exist levels of restraint and thoughts of reconsidering. In removing a pot from an anagama and taking notice of the incredible layers of ash and color it becomes apparent that showing restraint is sometimes the right decision. In many cases, the drawings on the pots were enough of a separation from the loose forms and the active surface. However, there also were pieces on which fire and ash had not sufficiently left their marks, and these pieces forced me to consider another layer.

It became interesting to find certain lines and shapes drawn on the surfaces, remaining intact and sustaining their crisp freshness. In others the drawings were intact, but only as a residual marking, subtle and ghostly.

Taking these pieces back into the studio meant the process continued. I included another layer, created using marks made by tiny brushes, and employing color from like containers of commercial glazes; a layer with a completely different sensibility and touch than the pot had seen thus far. In the electric kiln, earthy colors become more crisp, the Shinos richer and the commercial glazes brighter! The wood-fired pot that is refired in an oxidized atmosphere still emits the energy of flame and wood, but also is enhanced by the oxygen-rich atmosphere.

The additional layer to this process allows the surfaces of old and new, used and cherished to coexist. By combining retro with mingei and a touch of art deco with wabi-sabi, my intention has been to further consider the finality of a work.

Converting an Electric Kiln
for Wood or Gas Firing

by Bruce Bowers

Vase, 11 inches in height, thrown and altered stoneware, with Green Crackle Glaze, Orange and Black Slip, soda/wood fired to cone 11.

Covered jar, 11 inches in height, thrown, altered and carved stoneware, with Green Crackle Glaze, soda/wood fired to cone 11.

Those of us living in urban areas have limited access to firing in a fuel-burning kiln, because stringent zoning and fire regulations place severe limitations on our ability to build outdoor kilns near our homes. While many potters find a community college or local ceramics organization that has a gas or wood kiln, this situation often means turning your work over to someone else who is in strict control of this crucial part of the creative process. For more serious students, this situation can be less than satisfactory, but easily remedied.

When I taught at Hiram College in Hiram, Ohio, I could fire my pots in the college's gas kiln. This allowed me to experience all of the excitement, surprise and mystery of reduction firing. Later, when I moved to an urban area just outside of Washington, D.C., my only means of firing was in an electric kiln, and my work changed accordingly. Although this held my interest for a long time, I came to miss the adventure and the unexpected results that can come from firing in a fuel-burning kiln. Electric kilns are wonderful tools, but my creative needs

Bowl, 6½ inches in diameter, thrown and altered stoneware, with Shino Glaze and Black Slip, soda/wood fired to cone 11, by Bruce Bowers.

demanded another firing method. It was frustrating to think that my options were limited.

I started teaching at Glen Echo Pottery in Maryland. I am able to fire in a gas kiln again, and we also rent various wood kilns in rural areas. After becoming absolutely hooked on the wood-firing process, I began to think about how I could achieve some of the same effects on my own and with my students. As it turned out, the answer was right under my nose.

There were several old electric kilns in storage that we thought were beyond redemption. With encouragement from the pottery's director, we converted one of these old kilns to gas and added a stoke hole for wood. The entire conversion took about three hours. In my wildest dreams, I never thought the finished kiln would produce the results it has. We are able to get terrific flashing, ash buildup and, by adding a small amount of soda, a richness of surface that is usually reserved for pots produced in large, wood-fired kilns. As a matter of fact, I just had a group of pots fired in a big three-chambered wood kiln and, when I put these side

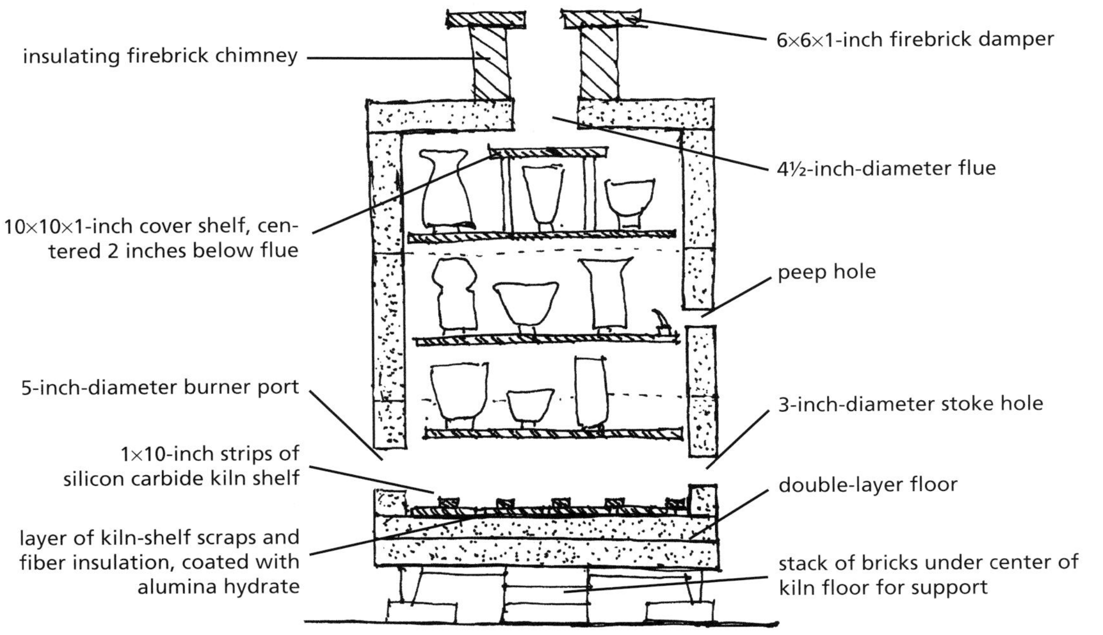

by side with my pots fired in the conversion kiln, I could hardly tell the difference.

The kiln conversion was virtually free. We used old silicon carbide shelves (sometimes broken ones), old posts and an existing propane burner on a flexible hose. Our only cost was a few dollars for kiln wash and clay to fill the old element grooves. Further, the kiln operates very efficiently, on less than 5 pounds of propane pressure, so the cost per firing is quite low.

This is an easy classroom project that involves students in the actual firing process. To get started, a simple ad placed in the newspaper or a flyer posted at your local pottery supplier could yield an old "beater" kiln just taking up room in someone's garage.

Our classes run in six-week sessions and we always fire our conversion kiln on the last day of the course. Each student is assigned a 20-minute stoking shift, and the entire class observes and participates in each phase of the firing. They cut and prepare the wood, prepare and stack the kiln, fire, and then unload and clean up. Students feel very much in touch with their finished pots, since they've paid careful attention to each part of the creative process.

Converting the Kiln

The bottom of the kiln was composed of two electric kiln bottoms sandwiched together. Broken shelves were then installed on top of this and the chinks between the shelves were filled with fiber insulation. This entire floor was then liberally sprinkled with alumina hydrate. Makeshift hobs, made of broken silicon carbide kiln shelves, were placed on the floor and braced by brick fragments. These keep the wood above the floor of the kiln to allow better air circulation and, as a result, better combustion. The firebox, therefore, occupies the bottom 5 inches of the kiln. Both gas and wood are introduced through the firebox.

All elements and electrical components were removed from the kiln, and the element grooves were filled with a very open clay body, composed of 50% fireclay and 50% sawdust by volume. Two holes were cut in the jacket and bricks, using a drill bit and a reciprocating saw. One hole is at six o'clock (burner port) and the other is at about one o'clock (stoke hole). A hole about 4 inches wide was cut in the lid, and a rudimentary chimney was made by placing four K23 insulating fire bricks on end to form an open rectangle. The outside of the lid and the area around the chimney were then covered with scraps of fiber insulation to inhibit excessive heat loss. A damper was made by simply placing two thin sections of insulating brick on top of the chimney.

All shelves, and the tops and bottoms of all posts, were liberally coated with a high-alumina kiln wash of 50 parts alumina hydrate, 25 parts silica and 25 parts EPK Kaolin. For wadding, we used 50 parts alumina hydrate and 50 parts EPK (all above measurements are by weight). The interior of the kiln, including the lid,

The burner for the conversion kiln is braced with brick on one side of the kiln, while the stoke hole for salt-soaked wood is on the other.

was coated with this same kiln-wash mixture.

It is important to emphasize that the shelves used in a kiln of this type should not be full rounds. We used sections of old broken silicon carbide shelves, leaving plenty of room for flame circulation around and up through the center of the setting.

It is also very important to place a "cover shelf" about 2 inches below the inside of the lid, above the stacked ware. This helps prevent a cold top section and also helps create thorough circulation of the flame. A 9×9-inch piece of silicon carbide shelf works well. We were able to get a temperature differential of less than one cone between the top and bottom of the kiln.

Gas and Wood

Our kiln is fired with propane gas using a model S-22 atmospheric Venturi burner, made by the Hauck Manufacturing Company in Lebanon, Pennsylvania. A flexible hose allows the burner to be used for our conversion kiln as well as for our main gas kiln. The converted kiln is fired with gas pressure from one pound to slightly over four pounds.

The gas burner is augmented by the inclusion of about 100 running feet of 1×2-inch pine (#2 pine). The wood is sawed into 1-foot lengths and soaked in a super-saturated solution of 1 pound of soda bicarbonate (baking soda) and one pound of sodium carbonate (soda ash) for about five days. By slowly adding these two chemicals to boiling water, it is easy to create a super-saturated solution. The wood is then dried in the sun. When done properly, a thin white residue will be visible on the surface of the boards. This technique allows the soda to be introduced very slowly and to naturally follow the direction of the flame and ash.

Also, 8 ounces (total) of fully saturated salt water is sprayed onto the last 25 lengths of wood, to be stoked after cone 9 is bending. This helps prevent totally dry areas on the pots.

Firing schedule

9 A.M. Open damper fully, turn gas to 1 pound of pressure and open primary air flange to produce a short, oxidizing flame.

10 A.M. The first blush of color is seen in the kiln atmosphere. The damper is still fully open and the gas is turned to 2.5 pounds of pressure. Primary air is opened slightly to continue with fully oxidizing flame.

11:30 A.M. cone 08 is down. The damper is closed slightly. The gas pressure is turned up to about 4 pounds. Primary air is cut back slightly. No blowback of flame at the burner port is visible at any point in the firing cycle. (We have had our best results when we forego a flame-deflecting brick inside of the burner port.) A distinctly orange flame about 6 inches long is consistently visible at the damper during this stage of clay body reduction. There is also slight backpressure at the bottom stoke hole and a lazy, hazy flame is traveling throughout the kiln. No smoke is visible.

12:30 P.M. The damper is almost fully open. Gas pressure is turned up to slightly less than 5 pounds. Primary air is opened a bit to create a neutral atmosphere. A short flame is visible at the damper (light orange with a slight greenish tinge). At this point, wood is added, one piece at a time, through the stoke hole. This activity immediately creates a reducing atmosphere and the stoke hole is quickly plugged with a piece of soft brick after each addition of wood. Pine burns with a long, somewhat lazy flame and its effects are immediately apparent in the kiln atmosphere. The kiln is allowed to clear completely to neutral before the next stoking. Cone 2 is reached at about 1 P.M.

1:30 P.M. cone 8 is just starting to bend. From this point on, we make virtually no adjustments to the gas pressure, the damper setting or the amount of primary air. We are simply firing with a neutral atmosphere (as far as the gas is concerned), and are falling into a pattern of alternating neutral and reducing atmospheres similar to those that one would achieve in a normal wood-fired kiln. Stoking of the soda-soaked (but dried) pine is increased to two pieces at a time. A moderate orange flame appears at the damper after each stoking. After letting the kiln atmosphere clear for about five minutes, we repeat the process.

2:30–4:30 P.M. All settings remain the same, except stoking increases to the rate of three pieces of pine about every five to seven minutes. This creates moderately heavy reduction with no smoke but with a strong orange flame about 12 inches high at the damper. The kiln clears to neutral and then is stoked again. cone 9 is down by 3 P.M. After 3 P.M., the same stoking frequency is maintained, but 8 ounces of fully saturated salt water is sprayed, using a plant mister, directly onto the pine just before stoking. This is repeated with each stoke cycle using only a small volume of the solution each time. The water vapor and the burning wood help distribute the salt along the path of the flame. Due to the high vapor pressure of salt, it migrates throughout the kiln very well. At 4:30, cone 10 is down and the main propane tank is turned off, the line to the burner is bled and the kiln is closed.

The temperature climb slows quite a bit during the last two hours. It is very easy to get to cone 8, but harder to get to cones 9 and 10. This is partially due to the increase in stoking and the accompanying reduction. It is also the result of firing in a kiln that was originally rated for cone 6–8. We are, therefore, pushing the insulating properties of the refractory bricks and are losing a lot of heat through the walls and lid. We estimate that, with proper care and religious kiln washing, this kiln should be able to withstand about 40 firings. Luckily, we have a few more abandoned kilns waiting for conversion and several offers of future donations. For people who love wood firing, but don't have ready access to a wood kiln, this project is a wonderful adventure.

Recipes

In our conversion kiln, we have our best results with light-colored, low-iron stoneware clay bodies. Porcelain also works very well, and can yield very handsome carbon trapping when hit directly by the soda. We find that higher-iron bodies tend to look muddy and exhibit very little flashing, unless covered with a white slip.

Orange Slip

Cone 10

Kentucky OM 4 Ball Clay	42.0 %
Avery Kaolin	42.0
Borax	5.4
Zircopax	10.6
	100.0 %

This slip flashes nicely on light clay bodies and produces color in the orange, red and tan range. It needs some soda or salt to look its best. Apply to leather-hard clay or bisqueware.

Shino Slip

Cone 10

Soda Ash	3.2 %
Nepheline Syenite	36.0
Soda Feldspar	8.6
Spodumene	12.2
Avery Kaolin	28.0
Kentucky OM 4 Ball Clay	12.0
	100.0 %

This flashes well on light-colored clay bodies, and produces colors in the white, tan and pink range. Apply to leather-hard clay or thinly to bisqueware.

Black Slip

Alberta Slip	60.6 %
Kentucky OM 4 Ball Clay	22.7
Chrome Oxide	7.5
Cobalt Carbonate	4.2
Red Iron Oxide	5.0
	100.0 %

This is an excellent decorating slip for brush work over bare clay or the Orange or Shino Slips above. It is very dark and looks best when used sparingly. Apply to leather-hard clay or thinly to bisqueware.

Shino Glaze

Cone 10

Soda Ash	4.0 %
Nepheline Syenite	45.0
Soda Feldspar	18.4
Spodumene	15.2
Ball Clay	15.0
EPK Kaolin	2.4
	100.0 %

This bleaches to a warm off-white when hit by soda or salt. It can be enhanced by sifting mixed hardwood ash over the damp glaze.

Green Crackle Glaze

Cone 10

Barium Carbonate	4.2 %
Whiting	13.0
Custer Feldspar	51.8
EPK Kaolin	4.2
Yellow Ocher	4.2
Silica	22.6
	100.0 %
Add: Bentonite	2.0 %
Epsom Salt	1.1 %

Mix Epsom salt in water before adding other materials. This is a dark waxy celadon that turns brilliant blue green when hit directly by heavy soda or salt.

Hamada Glaze

Cone 10

Red Iron Oxide	8.9 %
Whiting	15.5
Zinc Oxide	2.0
Custer Feldspar	41.1
EPK Kaolin	12.0
Silica	20.6
	100.0 %
Add: Bentonite	1.6 %

This glaze ranges from dark brown to black when used as a liner, and turns a runny amber when used on the exterior and directly hit by the soda.

Ten Basics of Firing

by Bill Jones

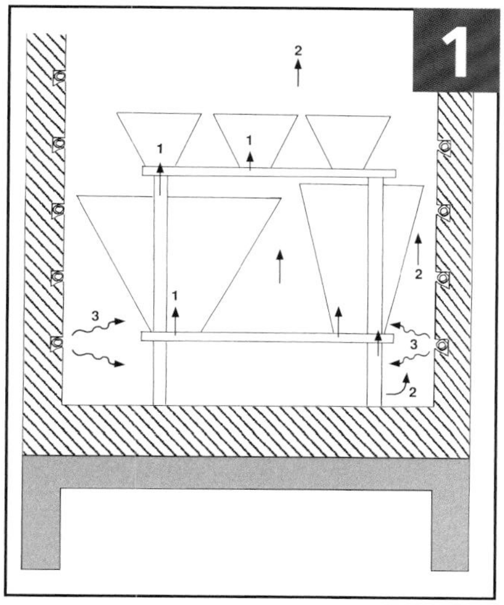

Firing is the most critical part of the ceramics process because it is the one thing that makes clay durable, hence ceramic. Here are some of the principles of firing and getting the best results with electric kilns.

From Mud to Ceramic

Firing converts ceramic work from weak clay into a strong, durable, crystalline glasslike form. Ceramic work is typically fired twice: it is bisque fired and then glaze fired. The goal of bisque firing is to convert greenware to a durable, semi-vitrified porous stage where it can be safely handled during the glazing and decorating process. It also burns out carbonaceous materials (organic materials in the clay, paper, etc.). As the temperature in a kiln rises, many changes take place in the clay. The Firing Chart (page 135) shows what happens to clay as it heats up.

More Science

Heat in an electric kiln is transferred in three ways (figure 1):

- conduction–heat transferred through physical contact (1)

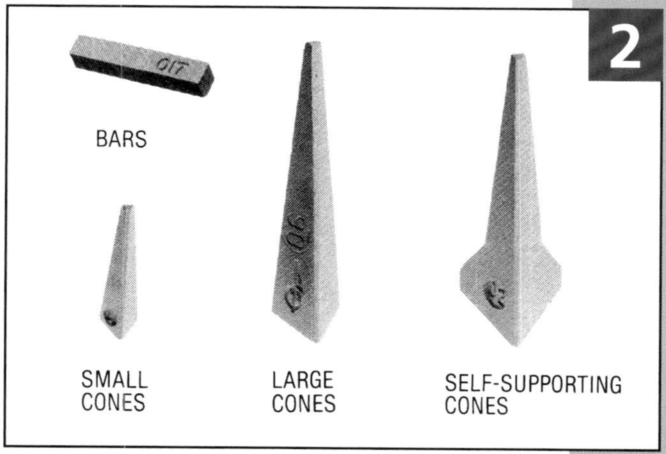

- convection–heat rising through the air (2)
- radiation–heat emanating from all the kiln elements (3).

Electricity passing through coiled heating elements (made especially for high temperatures) generates radiant heat, which rises and is absorbed by everything in the kiln.

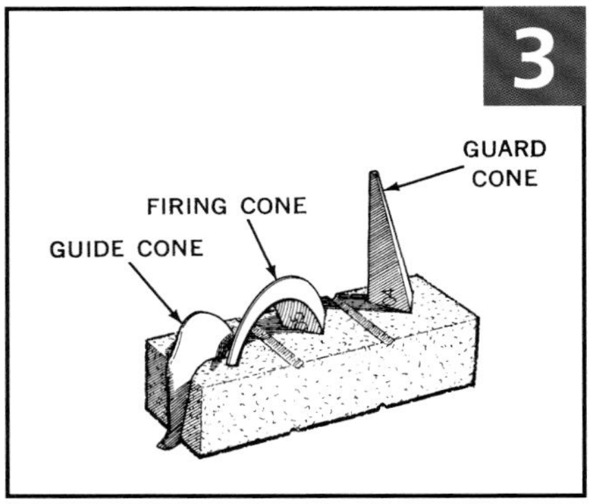

How Hot

All clays and glazes are formulated to mature at certain temperatures. Firing clay too high can cause it to deform or even melt, too low and it will not be durable. Firing glazes too high can cause run-off on the pot, too low and they will be dry and rough. To fire to the right temperature, pyrometric cones are used. Cones are made from various oxide mixtures and bend at known temperatures (figure 2). In general, the following cones are used in the pottery studio: bisque fire (cone 08–05), low fire (cone 06–04), mid-range (cone 4–7) and high fire (cone 8–10).

Using Cones

Cones are used in every firing. Typically, a three-cone system (either large or self-supporting), consisting of a guide cone that is one cone below the target temperature, the firing cone and a guard cone (figure 3) provides the best information about the firing. Bar cones and small cones are used in a properly adjusted Kiln-Sitter®, an automatic shut-off device (figure 4). While the three large cones are not required for kilns equipped with a KilnSitter or an automatic controller, they do provide a second point of reference for how a kiln is operating.

Get Ready

Before firing any kiln, vacuum it out if necessary—bottom, sides, element channels and lid. Check the el-

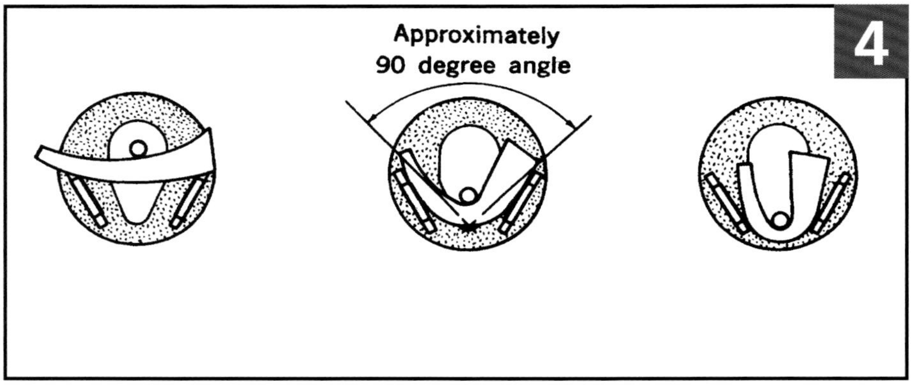

ements for breaks, and chisel off any glaze drips on the shelves. Visually check the electrical cords and connections. Make any repairs required (see owners manual or call your local supplier for service).

Kiln Furniture

An assortment of kiln furniture (figure 5) is needed to hold and support ware during a firing. Furniture consists of shelves, posts, stilts and tile setters made from refractory materials. Kiln furniture is designed to withstand the repeated heating and cooling to high temperatures without deforming.

The Bisque Load

Loading a bisque kiln is a fairly simple task, but there are some basic rules. Fire full loads to take advantage of conduction heating and also save electricity. All work should be bone dry . If the work is cool or cold to the touch, it is not bone dry. Handle all work very carefully because it is extremely fragile at this stage. Place the bottom shelf on 1-inch stilts to aid circulation, and keep ware 1 inch away from elements, walls, thermocouple and KilnSitter (figure 6). Unglazed pieces may touch each other. Place a small cone in the KilnSitter and/or a cone pad on the middle shelf. Fire to cone 08–05, depending on the type of clay and amount of porosity you want for glazing.

The Bisque Fire

During the bisque firing a lot of damage can take place. Thicker pieces with moisture or air bubbles create the biggest problem. Clay needs to dry evenly through its entire thickness. If the outside dries faster, it seals off the escape route for the interior moisture. The interior moisture turns to steam and forces its way out (explodes) during the bisque. To avoid this, start off slowly when firing a bisque kiln. Turn on one element to low. If you do not have a downdraft exhaust system, prop the lid open, take the peephole plugs out and keep the temperature below 212°F until all the moisture is gone. Close the lid and check for moisture (hold a mirror or piece of glass up to the top peephole to see if it fogs up). Turn on all elements to low for at

Kiln Controllers

Many electric kilns are now equipped with kiln controllers. Kiln controllers use a signal from a thermocouple (a sensing device that detects temperature) that's located in the kiln. When the controller senses the temperature, it compares this information with a computer program that tells the relays to turn on or off. The relays control current going to the elements. Controllers take the guesswork out of when and how high to turn up the heat on the kiln. Because they are accurate at sensing temperature, they are more efficient than manually-fired kilns. They come with preset programs, or you can even easily input programs to adjust to special firing requirements.

Safety

Firing is a potentially hazardous activity and all students must obey safety rules to avoid injury. Instructors must read and understand all the safety information that came with the kiln, and assure that the kiln is properly installed and maintained. If a manual is not available, many companies post them online or you can request a replacement copy from the manufacturer. For operating the kiln, students must:

- Turn off kiln prior to loading or unloading. Disconnect the kiln for any servicing or when kiln is not in use.
- Do not touch heating elements with anything since they carry high voltage.
- Do not place any combustibles within 12 inches of any surface of the kiln.
- Do not leave kiln unattended while firing.
- Never look into a hot kiln without properly tinted safety glasses (e.g., welder's glasses). Sunglasses only block ultraviolet light.
- Make sure the ventilation system is working properly.
- Never add extra insulation around a kiln to conserve energy. Extra insulation can cause the wiring and the steel case to overheat.
- Remove all tripping hazards. Keep the power cord out of the way.
- Do not fire with cracked shelves. They can break during firing, which could damage the ware inside the kiln. Store kiln shelves in a dry area.
- If you smell burning plastic, turn the kiln off. Examine the wall outlet and power cord for signs of burning.
- Never wear loose-fitting clothing around a hot kiln.
- Do not open a kiln until it has cooled to room temperature. Pots may break from thermal shock.
- Keep the kiln closed when not in use, and never place anything on the kiln lid, even when the kiln is idle—you may forget.
- Always keep unsupervised children away from the kiln.
- Do not place any objects under or around the kiln stand. Blocking airflow changes the kiln's heating characteristics.
- Remove all flammable materials from the kiln room.

least an hour then to medium for an hour before turning all elements on to high. The firing is done when the firing cone falls.

The Glaze Fire

Vacuum the kiln, especially if any pieces exploded during the bisque. When firing glazed pieces, make sure there is a thin coating of kiln wash (available from suppliers) on the shelves (figure 7). You do not need a fresh coat for each firing, but any bare spots should be coated. Built-up kiln wash becomes bumpy and should be cleaned off with a chisel. All glazed pieces must be checked to make sure there is no glaze touching the shelf. Coat with wax at least ½inch from the bottom of the piece. Sort work by height and place on shelves with a minimum of ½ inch between pieces and 1 inch from the walls, elements and KilnSitter. Turn the kiln on low for about an hour and then medium for about an hour before turning on to high. The higher the cone you are going to, the longer it will take to fire.

What's That Smell?

Clay and ceramic materials change their chemistry when fired. Carbonaceous materials burn out between 500°F–1450°F. Firing clay materials in electric and gas kilns produces carbon monoxide, formaldehyde, sulfur dioxide gases and more. Some of the byproducts are harmful so vent kilns to the outside. A downdraft vent system works best, but an updraft or crossdraft system is better than nothing. All kilns must be vented to the outdoors.

Kiln Checkup

by Bill Jones

With the beginning of fall, ceramic activities reach a heightened pace: schools are back in session, art centers are gearing up and studios are moving into full production for the holiday season. Jeopardizing your firing schedule due to a preventable problem will provide you with a regrettable head-slapping "doh" moment. Since wear and tear on a kiln is associated more with the level of use rather than any span of time, a yearly checkup is the least you can do to set your mind at ease. If you're firing more than a few times a month, more frequent checkups are necessary.

Temperature Control Devices

Temperature control devices are one of the most important parts of the kiln. While no kiln should be fired unattended, assurance that your control devices are in good working order should be a top priority. Always monitor your kiln's accuracy by using pyrometric cones on the shelf. For kilns with a Dawson KilnSitter, inspect and clean the tube assembly and replace the sensing rod if worn, then calibrate the weight and claw adjustment. For computer controllers, check thermocouple screw connections at the porcelain block.

Switches and Relays

Basically, there are two types of kiln controllers used to control the temperature in a kiln. Kilns with kiln sitters use switches and those with controllers use relays. Since it's difficult to predict when a switch will need to be replaced, always keep a spare on hand. For relays, they need to be replaced every year under heavy use, and less often for lighter use. Inspect connections and tighten screws that hold the tabs. If the connectors are loose, replace them, do not pinch them to make them tighter as this can distort the contact area.

Plug and Receptacle

Check the plug and receptacle. If the prongs are bright brass color, you're in good shape. If they appear brown or black, have a qualified electrician replace both the plug and receptacle.

Elements

Brick dust and glaze particles can settle in the element grooves causing elements to wear out faster. Vacuum the elements before each firing to increase their lifespan. As elements wear, firings take longer and eventually your kiln will stall out. Keeping a log of how long it takes to fire a kiln will provide an indication of element wear. When replacing elements, replace all of them at once.

Venting System

Test downdraft venting systems by holding a match or stick of incense just above the intake holes in the lid. The smoke or flame should be drawn down through the holes. If it isn't, then there may be a problem with the ductwork or the vent itself. Inspect the ductwork for possible leaks or obstructions, especially if you smell fumes during the firing. Patch any leaks with duct tape.

Bands and Lid

Inspect the stainless steel bands that compress the bricks in your kiln. Tighten the hose clamp connectors at least once a year. This will prevent excessive movement of the bricks against each other as the kiln expands and contracts with heating and cooling. Also, check that the lid mounting screws are snug but be careful since the threads will strip if overtightened.

Need Maintenance Information?

For maintenance, begin with your owners manual. Since these have often been lost or misplaced, you'll be able to find help on the websites of the kiln manufacturers. Many of them have owner's manuals that are downloadable in PDF format, and using the search functions on their sites will get you where you need to go. If you can't find what you need by searching, contact the manufacturer by email and be sure to include the make and model number of your kiln, along with any other identifying information such as the type of KilnSitter or controller. Many times, you'll find the personnel at your local ceramics supply store are capable of diagnosing, maintaining and repairing any type of kiln.

The Oxidation Reverberation

by Jayne Shatz

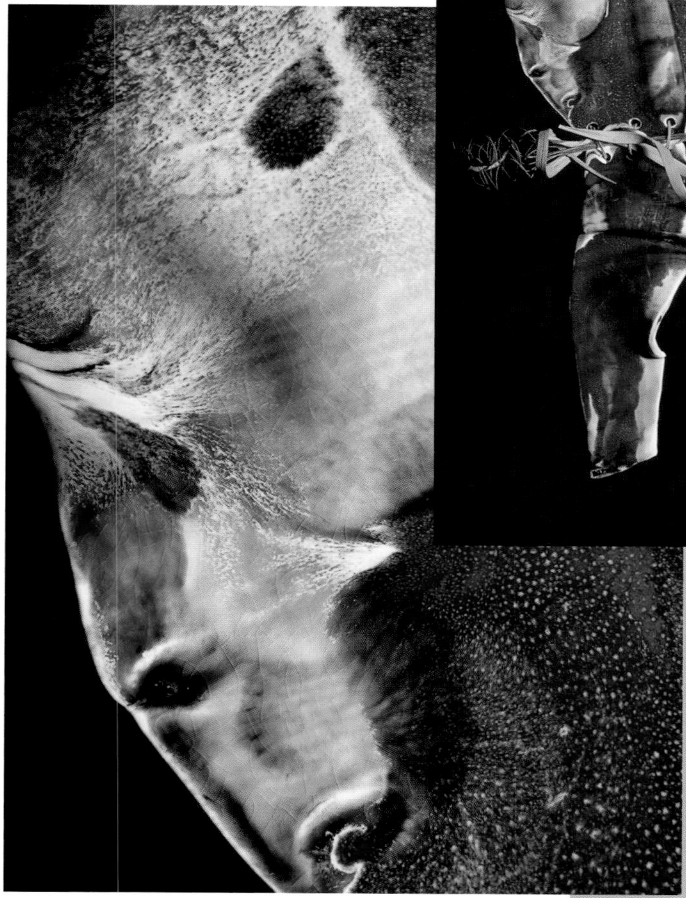

PHOTOS: STANLEY BLANCHARD

"Barcelona," 4 feet in height, porcelain, with Clear, Blue Matt, Costello Carbonate and Rutile Matt glazes.

A society's identity is distinguished by its art. The political, economical and environmental climate influences daily life. Consequently, the artistic milieu of a culture is echoed through the shared thoughts and visions of its people embracing the arts.

I embarked upon my career during a time of tumultuous dissent. It was the early 1970s and the U.S. was embroiled in Vietnam. Everyone was protesting something. All the rules were changing, and I was striving to grow up. I moved into a commune with three people I had met at the State University of New York at Albany and began my long love affair with clay. We built an 80-cubic-foot gas kiln, furnished a studio and enthusiastically launched the Kilnhaus Pottery. We sold cone 10 reduction-fired stoneware and porcelain from home, from a shopping mall gallery, as well as wholesale. We were making a living, and living off our art!

When we were students, our university had wonderful equipment and funding. We turned the burners on and out came gas! Then everything changed. In October of 1973, the Organization of the Petroleum Exporting Countries (OPEC) stopped exporting oil to the United States and other Western nations. Gasoline prices quadrupled. One week during the crisis, up to 20% of the country's gas stations had no fuel.

My friends and I were middle-class baby boomers from Long Island and Queens. We came from comfortable homes, never experiencing

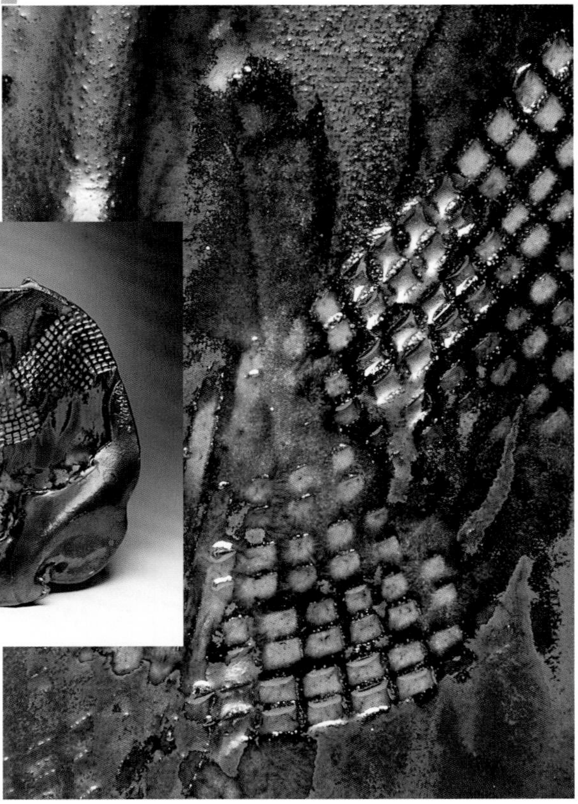

"Zen Plate," 22 inches in height, stoneware, with Matt Black and Blue Matt glazes.

"need," but the energy crisis filtered down into almost everything we did. Thermostats plummeted, roadway speed limits were lowered and small economy cars were produced by the automobile industry. The cost of propane for firing our kiln skyrocketed. Gasoline prices made travel problematic, and we became very selective of the shows in which we participated. We made crucial decisions about heating a large studio during nonworking hours. We had clays and glazes that would freeze during the harsh winters, so we moved them into our house at night and brought them back into the studio the next day. Fortunately, we were young and strong. We continued working in our craft and sought additional means of financial support. We opened our studio to the public and held classes. The increased exposure to the community elevated our pottery sales and Kilnhaus Pottery remained successful.

When I moved into the city in 1976, I was forced to "go electric." At that time, my contemporaries looked down on electric kilns and oxidation glazes. After all, we were hurly-burly, brick-and-burner, reduction-fired gas guzzlers! But all that was changing. I had to make my way in a strange new world. Having built three large outdoor brick kilns, I felt I was committing a despicable act by purchasing an electric kiln. It was stainless steel, shiny and fit into a corner of my basement studio. I had no clay bodies, glazes or low-temperature experience. I bought this kiln because it had the potential of firing up to cone 10. But I soon asked myself, "Why bother firing up to cone 10 when cone 6 would be more cost effective?" After all, it wasn't the temperature range that was so cataclysmic; it was the fact that I was switching over from reduction to oxidation. That was the whole ballgame. Ultimately, I committed to working at cone 6 in oxidation, and recreating the glazes I was accustomed to using at cone 10 in reduction.

I surveyed this problem in its most rudimentary components. Simply speaking, a reduction clay body develops its toasty warm color when the oxygen entering the kiln is reduced by closing down the kiln's dampers.

"Pedestal Bowl," 12 inches in height, stoneware, Glossy Black over Blue Matt glaze.

This reduction of oxygen and increase in carbon creates the autumnal colors of reduction stoneware.

I read everything I could on clay bodies and clay chemistry. I finally developed a cone 6 clay body that was rich in iron and would develop into a toasty warm color in oxidation.

Then I began bringing down the melting temperatures of my glazes to cone 6. I delved further into chemistry, learning the various effects oxides produced in an oxidizing atmosphere. Very slowly, and with many glaze tests, I began to obtain the colors I was seeking. My first success was to duplicate an iron saturated glaze from my college days, Ketchup Red. I then continued down my palette of glazes. This process took two years. I continued selling pottery during this time, which meant that, for a long time, I was working with only one glaze. Fortunately, people were buying my pots.

By the time I started on adjusting my porcelain, I was quite knowledgeable about cone 6 oxidation chemicals and atmospheric conditions. However, trying to learn about midrange porcelain was like beating my head against a stone wall. No one knew anything about it. There was very little information. I felt as if I were back in the ninth century, trying to sieze the precious secret of the Chinese porcelains!

Painstakingly, I developed a white porcelain clay body with which I was satisfied. It was not translucent, but that was not a quality I was pursuing. Because of this characteristic, and the midrange temperature, there is some debate over whether or not it is truly porcelain. For me, it is a clay body that is beautifully white, dense, nonbrittle and throws fantastically. The body contains bentonite, enabling it to be plastic and very strong. It even can be once

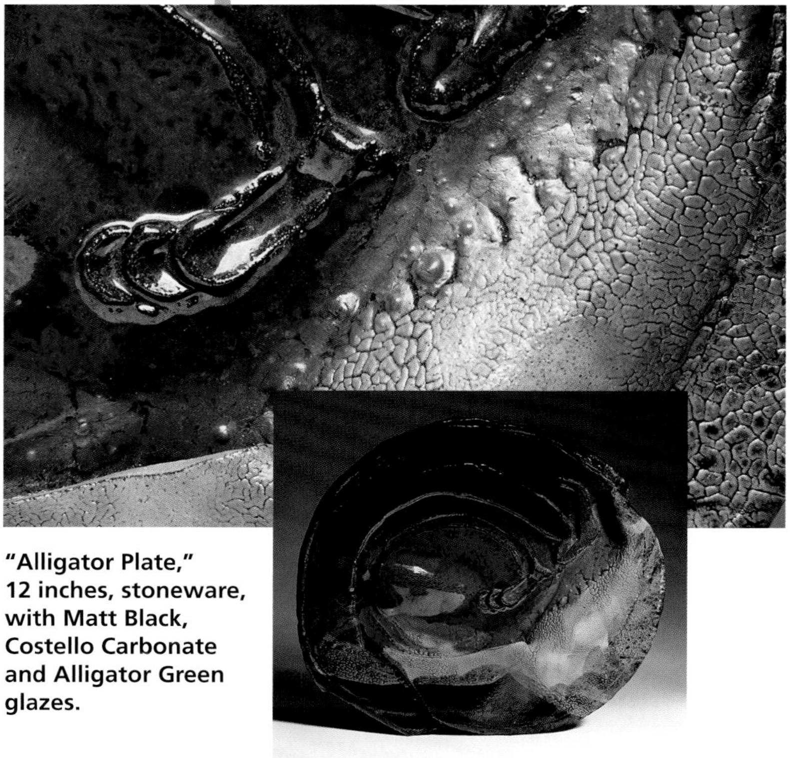

"Alligator Plate," 12 inches, stoneware, with Matt Black, Costello Carbonate and Alligator Green glazes.

fired. I found out years after I developed the body that my clay distributor believed it to be one of the best slip-casting bodies he had ever used. It is now used by several tile and slip-casting companies for industry. I can be very casual with it, due to its plasticity and strength, and it is fabulous for large sculptural pieces. With the addition of sand, it becomes an excellent white raku body.

After much work, I produced a wonderful clear glaze for my porcelain. It was very clean on the surface and pooled into crevices, where it transformed into a lovely robin's egg blue. It reminded me of the beautiful "Scarab Vase" by Adelaide Alsop Robineau. If you look closely at that pot, the pooled areas are a lovely soft blue. This realization hit me like a thunderbolt! What I should have done so many years ago was research the glazes of American Art Pottery. Ironically, many of those potteries worked in oxidation. The answers were there; I just didn't know where to look.

I discovered that, by layering glazes, I could achieve certain cone 10 reduction effects. I learned to work with base glazes, varying the oxides to make additional glazes.

The years progressed and it seemed the entire country was firing electric. Kilns got better, clay and glaze recipes filled books and publications, and the Internet was born. Oxidation firing in American ceramics flourished.

Developing a cone 6 palette was an enormous struggle, but I learned a great deal about clay and glazes. I extended that knowledge into a lifetime of teaching and have derived great pleasure in sharing my recipes. During my thirty-odd years in clay, wonderful people have shared with me their time, glazes, studios and hearts.

Just as majolica was born out of Europe's quest for Chinese porcelain, America's energy crisis birthed a method that has made an indelible mark on the landscape of contemporary ceramics. This voyage reinforces our responsibility as ceramists to broaden the American ceramics tradition and preserve its voice in the vast continuum of ceramics history.

Recipes

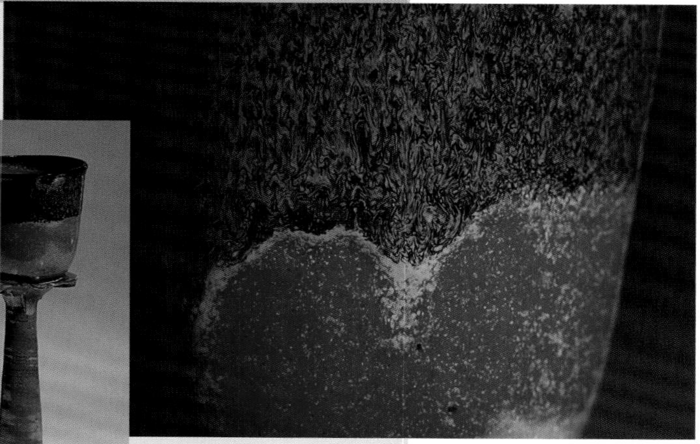

"Goblet," 12 inches in height, stoneware, with Ketchup Red under Glossy Black to create a hare's fur pattern, by Jayne Shatz.

Shatz Stoneware

Cone 6

A.P. Green Fire Clay	25.0 %
Cedar Heights Redart	6.0
Jordan Clay	40.0
Tennessee Ball Clay #5	21.0
Silica	8.0
	100.0 %
Add: Burnt Umber	4.0 %

Gorgeous, dark chocolate brown. An excellent throwing body.

Shatz Porcelain

Cone 6

Nepheline Syenite	26.0 %
EPK Kaolin	38.0
Jackson Ball Clay	10.0
Silica	26.0
	100.0 %
Add: Bentonite	4.0 %

Fantastic strong body, good for large-scale work. It is not translucent, but is excellent for throwing. Add white sand for a raku body.

Rutile Matt

Cone 6

Whiting	20.0 %
Nepheline Syenite	56.0
EPK Kaolin	18.0
Silica	6.0
	100.0 %
Add: Rutile	7.0 %
Zinc Oxide	9.0 %

A beautiful, soft, tan matt, this glaze pools creamy white where thick.

Blue Matt

Cone 6

Dolomite	7.2 %
Gerstley Borate	11.3
Talc	13.9
Nepheline Syenite	39.1
EPK Kaolin	9.5
Silica	19.0
	100.0 %
Add: Cobalt Carbonate	1.0 %
Cobalt Oxide	1.0 %
Rutile	6.0 %

Ketchup Red

Cone 6

Gerstley Borate	31.0 %
Talc	14.0
Custer Feldspar	20.0
EPK Kaolin	5.0
Silica	30.0
	100.0 %
Add: Spanish Red Iron Oxide	15.0 %

Recipes

Glossy Black

Cone 6

Gerstley Borate	10.7 %
Whiting	5.5
Custer Feldspar	78.9
EPK Kaolin	4.9
	100.0 %
Add: Cobalt Oxide	2.1 %
Copper Carbonate	4.1 %
Manganese Dioxide	4.1 %

Rich black with silvery highlights where thick. For hare's fur pattern, layer over Ketchup Red.

Matt Black

Cone 6

Barium Carbonate	18.4 %
Gerstley Borate	8.0
Custer Feldspar	36.8
Barnard Clay	18.4
EPK Kaolin	9.2
Silica	9.2
	100.0 %
Add: Cobalt Oxide	2.3 %
Copper Oxide	3.4 %
Iron Oxide	2.3 %
Zinc Oxide	9.2 %

Alligator Green

Cone 6

Barium Carbonate	7.6 %
Gerstley Borate	18.5
Talc	6.5
Whiting	2.1
Custer Feldspar	41.3
Silica	24.0
	100.0 %
Add: Copper Carbonate	6.8 %
Zinc Oxide	8.7
Zircopax	86.9

Clear Base Glaze

Cone 6

Barium Carbonate	8.7 %
Gerstley Borate	25.0
Whiting	8.7
Custer Feldspar	38.0
Silica	19.6
	100.0 %
Add: Bentonite	8.7 %
Glossy White (great liner glaze)	
Zircopax	13.0 %
Apple Green Celadon	
Copper Carbonate	1.0 %
Jade Green	
Copper Carbonate	3.2 %

Costello Carbonate

Cone 6

Barium Carbonate	6.0 %
Gerstley Borate	20.0
Whiting	2.0
Custer Feldspar	45.0
Tennessee Ball Clay	2.0
Silica	25.0
	100.0
Add: Copper Carbonate	6.0 %

This is beautiful when used with Rutile Matt as a decorative addition.

Color and Texture

by Jonathan Kaplan

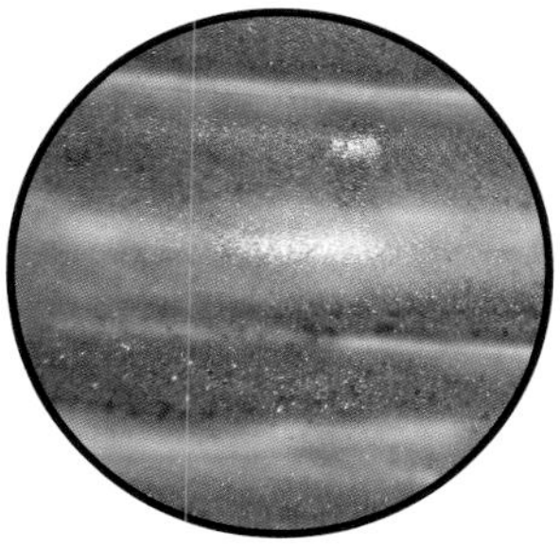

"Vase with Circular Attributes and Stand" 15 inches in height, with Edgy Green glaze. This glaze contains barium, which helps in the formation of small suspended crystals giving it a satin matt finish.

Color and texture in cone 6 glazes are the result of three variables: First, selecting proper glazes; second, learning how to layer and combine different glazes by pouring, dipping and spraying; and third, using a controlled cooling cycle to further enhance the color and texture. This slow cooling not only creates a visual dialog in thick and thin areas of glaze application, but also helps with the crystallization of certain materials, which adds depth and interest to the glaze.

Glaze Selection

With so many cone 6 glazes, how do you know which glazes will work for you? It's impossible to look at a written glaze formula and know how it will look when it's fired and cooled. However, there are some things to look for that may provide some insight as to the surface texture. I like to use glazes that have a strong presence of calcium, provided by whiting and wollastonite in the formula. Dolomite, which is a combination in equal parts of both calcium and magnesium is also very helpful. These materials, when included in any glaze along with other ceramic materials, form small, suspended crystals in the glaze when cooled in a controlled manner.

Glaze Application

I spray or dip glazes over each other. My experience is that no single glaze can provide a visually interesting surface in an electric kiln, although there may certainly be exceptions. My layering technique allows the many differing glaze materials to combine and melt in unique ways providing a visually interesting surface with depth. All of this is caused by the interactions of multiple materials applied over each other. Applying glazes over textures in the clay allows the melted glaze to pool. A thicker concentration of glaze materials in these areas yields different areas of color.

When mixing and testing glazes for future use on your pottery, it is useful to try different methods of combining glazes. For example, if you mix up a few small test batches of different glazes, try dipping one

NOTE

Always test new glazes before committing them to your finished work!

Recipes

PV Base
Cone 6

Gerstley Borate	30.0 %
Whiting	10.0
PV Clay	15.0
Custer Feldspar	35.0
Silica	10.0
	100.0 %
Black liner glaze	
Add: Mason 6600	6.0 %

An excellent gloss base. Spray or dip over Blue/Green/Purple. This glaze is very receptive to commercial stains. Again, with encapsulated stains, an opacifier is not necessary. If a more opaque surface is desired, add between 6–10% opacifier such as Zircopax.

VC Glaze
Cone 6

Whiting	6.9 %
Gerstley Borate	11.6
Titanium Dioxide	6.9
Nepheline Syenite	46.8
Kaolin	13.9
Silica	13.9
	100.0 %
Blue/Green/Purple variation	
Add: Cobalt Oxide	1.1%

An excellent base glaze to spray or dip other glazes on top.

Edgy Green
Cone 6

Barium Carbonate	15.6 %
Gerstley Borate	10.4
Wollastonite	15.6
Nepheline Syenite	39.7
Kaolin	10.4
Silica	8.3
	100.0 %
Add: Black Copper Oxide	3.1 %

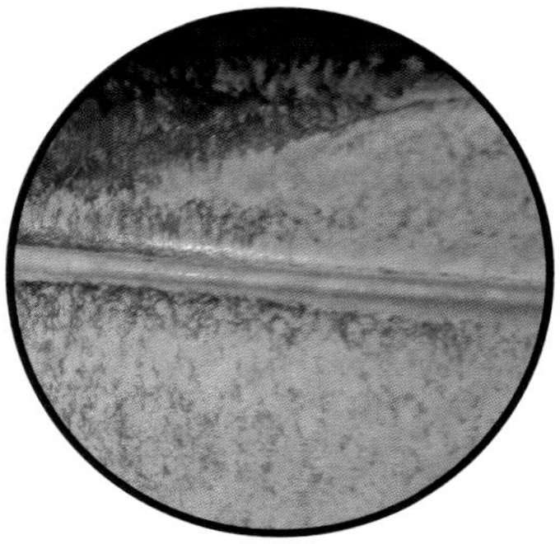

"Disk Vase," 18 inches in height, with Blue/Green/Purple variation of VC Glaze with PV Black sprayed over. The detail shows the cooling crystals that developed during a controlled slow cooling.

glaze over the other on the top rim of your test tile. Then reverse the order. For instance, if you dip glaze A over glaze B, then do another tile with glaze B dipped over glaze A.

Firing

Most glazes have a range of several cones. I fire my cone 6 glazes to cone 7 using a programmable controller with the following heating and cooling cycle:

1st segment........50°F/hour to 220°F

2nd segment........250°F/hour to 2167°F

3rd segment........150°F/hour to 1500°F

I have found that this provides a better melt and allows a good mingling of the many layers of glaze. It's necessary to experiment and test your glazes to determine their range. Using kiln wash on the shelves or stilts under your ware is a necessity!

You can program a "hold" into the end of the second segment if you have a single zone kiln and wish to try to even out the firing from top to bottom. With the introduction of multiple zone controls on many of the new kilns, a soak at the end is not really necessary. If you don't have a computer-controlled kiln, use the infinite switches to "fire down" the kiln. With the addition of a pyrometer and a decent thermocouple, you can achieve a reasonable controlled cooling cycle.

Record Keeping

Keep accurate records so you can repeat pleasing results. In an electric kiln this is easy, especially if it is equipped with a programmable controller. There is no substitute for experimenting. It takes time and persistence to achieve the surfaces that are pleasing to you. No one glaze or method will work. It is a combination of glazes and applications, followed by the proper firing with a controlled cooling cycle.

Designing with Wax Resist

by Marj Peeler

Round pot, white low-fire clay with wax-resist design, fired to cone 05.

Glaze and wax don't mix—how fortunate for potters! Wax resist serves a variety of practical purposes—from keeping the bottom of a pot from sticking to the kiln shelf to allowing you to fire the bottom and lid of a covered pot together—anywhere you want to repel glaze.

You can use wax resist for artistic purposes, too. Some potters like to splatter wax on the bisque before dipping it into the glaze, hoping an appealing, free form design will emerge from the kiln. Others like to use a well-thought-out design when decorating with wax resist. This process will leave bare clay lines contrasting with the glazed areas, which can be spectacular with the right combination of clay and glaze color. The range of designs is practically unlimited.

The Process

You'll need a few basic materials to place the design on the pot (figure 1). Since wax resist that's clear when dry is hard to see when applied to bisque, add a few drops of food coloring to the wax to help solve this problem. You'll also need a selection of brushes—a brush with long, narrow bristles that works well for painting thin lines, and others of varying size and thickness, depending on your design and the size of the lines.

Your design can be simple, complex, abstract or realistic, all depending on your ability, inspiration and the surface you're covering (figure 2). The geometric design used for this project was based on a circle divided into eight equal parts. You'll improve your chance of success by planning and sketching before placing your design on the pot.

Place your pot on a banding wheel and carefully draw your design with a pencil (figure 3). The pencil lines will burn out during firing. Divide the design into eight parts and draw lines from the center to each of the eight points. Draw in the other lines needed to complete the design.

Slowly and carefully, using the narrow pointed brush, paint the wax resist over the pencil lines (figure 4). You may need some practice to gain control over this technique. Try working on some blank paper before attempting it on the pot.

TIP

You can use hot water and liquid soap to remove most of the wax from your brushes. I've found that using a little lacquer thinner on the brush after washing it in water removes any remaining residue.

TIP

If small particles of glaze adhere to the waxed areas, carefully remove them using the end of a wooden tool or toothpick. You might try using a Q-Tip to clean these areas. I usually wet the cotton tip slightly when doing this step.

A sample of the materials needed for the wax-resist technique.

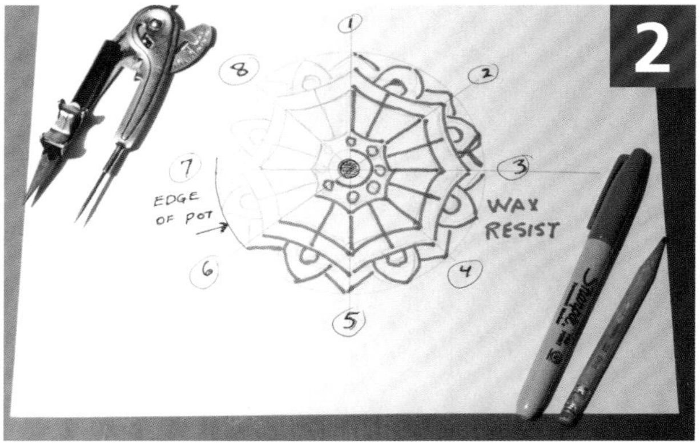

Plan and sketch your design before starting a project.

Using a banding wheel, draw the design on the pot with a pencil.

Carefully cover the pencil lines with the wax resist.

After the wax resist has dried, apply the glaze by dipping, brushing or spraying. You may need to apply several coats to obtain the correct thickness for the glaze surface, depending on the density of your bisqueware.

Fire the pot to the appropriate temperature for your clay and glazes. Glazes that tend to flow when fired should be avoided when using this wax-resist technique.

CAUTION

If you make a mistake, you need to re-bisque the pot and start over. The wax soaks into the surface of the ware and can only be removed by firing it again. If you do not want to refire, you might try to work the mistake into the design.

After glazing the pot, clean away the excess glaze with a tool.

Wood-Ash Glazing at Cone 6

by Harry Spring

Round vase, 9 inches in height, white stoneware, with slip trailing, blue Wood Ash Glaze over Green Dragon Matt Glaze, fired to cone 6 in oxidation.

High firing in a gas kiln for many years does have a downside. You can come to depend upon the kiln to give you the wonderful, serendipitous effects that are part of the magic of reduction. Of course, we all know that wonderful glazes can also be achieved without reducing the kiln's atmosphere. Several years ago, I was forced through circumstances to use an electric kiln as my only firing source for my line of production stoneware. Since then, I have not only come to "put up" with electric firing and the challenges of a static kiln atmosphere, but also to appreciate the convenience of electronically controlled kilns and the challenge of discovering ways of developing interesting and even exciting glaze effects.

I began by testing several commercial clays, and settled on a white stoneware (Miller 65) that was both durable and totally vitrified at cone 6. Available through Laguna Clay Company, it is good for throwing small- to medium-sized pieces, weighing 1 to 10 pounds.

I then experimented with ways to develop more interesting surfaces. I tried carving patterns into the clay to create places where the glaze could flow and pool. Another technique that I learned from a friend in California was to take the slurry from my throwing bucket, run it through a 60- to 80-mesh sieve and apply it with an ear syringe for trailed-slip patterning.

Next, I tried overlapping two and three glazes to create some movement on the surface. This worked

Vase, 9 inches in height, white stoneware, with blue Wood Ash Glaze over Green Dragon Matt Glaze, fired to cone 6 in oxidation.

Small round vase, 6 inches in height, with wood ash sieved on Green Wood Ash Glaze over Green Dragon Matt Glaze, fired to cone 6 in oxidation, by Harry Spring.

wonderfully, but caused some irregularities where the glaze saturated the bisqueware, and some running onto the kiln shelves when the glaze application was too thick. I found I could control the application thickness more easily and avoid running by spraying the second and third coats of glaze.

Most recently, I have begun using wood ash in and over my Cone 6 glazes to create visual interest. The results have been very exciting. I was fortunate to find a recipe that does not require washing the ash before adding it to the glaze. Of course, this makes a glaze that is somewhat caustic, but I wear surgical gloves when I glaze anyway, so this has not been a problem.

I have found that this recipe works best if it is dipped or sprayed over another glaze; alone, it is a little too dry to the touch. I like using Wood Ash Glaze over a matt glaze rather than a gloss glaze.

To prepare the wood ash, screen the dry ash (any wood will do) through a 60- to 80-mesh sieve and add it to the glaze batch.

Another way to achieve interesting effects is to simply sieve wood ash over the damp, newly glazed surface. I do this over a trash barrel. (Remember: ash is caustic, so always wear a mask.)

For the most dramatic effects, do both. Sieve the dry wood ash over the rim and shoulder of a pot that has just been sprayed with Wood Ash Glaze over a dipped or sprayed base glaze, such as Green Dragon Matt Glaze.

Wood ash contains a good deal of calcium, as well as potassium, phosphorus, magnesium and sodium—all rather active fluxes in a glaze—so I limit the application of Wood Ash Glaze to the top fourth of the pot.

Recipes

Green Dragon Matt Glaze

Cone 6

Whiting	17.7 %
Zinc Oxide	8.0
Cornwall Stone	22.0
Soda Feldspar	44.1
Bentonite	3.2
EPK Kaolin	5.0
	100.0 %
Add: Titanium Dioxide	4.0 %
Copper Carbonate	4.3 %

Frasca Wood Ash Glaze

Cone 6

Whiting	11.4 %
Wood Ash (unwashed)	54.6
Potash Feldspar	11.3
Ball Clay	11.3
Silica	11.4
	100.0 %
Green	
Add: Copper Carbonate	4.0 %
Blue	
Add: Cobalt Carbonate	2.0 %

A Wood-Fired Look

by Richard Busch

Bowl, 2½ inches in height, thrown and faceted stoneware, with brushed stain and layered glazes, fired to cone 6.

Like most people who take up pottery, I was limited at the beginning of my career to firing my pots to cone 6 in an electric kiln. This was at the local community center where I lived in northern Virginia. I say limited, but for the first year or so it didn't seem like a limitation. Just learning to center, make simple forms and digest a lot of basic information about the pottery process was enough to keep my focus pretty narrow. But it wasn't too long before I began to notice the differences between oxidation- and reduction-fired pottery.

A few years later, I took a wood-firing workshop with McKenzie Smith at Baltimore Clayworks. Out of that kiln—which we fired to cone 10 in about 14 hours, throwing in some salt around cone 8—came some of the warmest, toastiest, most wonderfully earthy and handsome pots I'd ever seen. It was inspiring. It changed my outlook. I was hooked on the whole idea. But then, not seeing any possibility of doing wood/salt myself on a regular basis, I grew frustrated.

If, as they say, necessity is the mother of invention, I would suggest that frustration can also be that mother. At least it was for me. Out of that sense of frustration came the desire to develop a cone 6 oxidation glaze that would yield the wood/salt-fired look that had become something of an obsession.

So I started playing around with glaze recipes and, after awhile, came up with something that filled the bill—until I finally built the salt kiln I'd been planing for a long time.

Not only did my ersatz wood/salt-glazing technique keep me happy for years of electric-kiln firing, it also fooled a lot of people, including some pretty experienced potters—at least at first glance. Of course, when they picked up a pot and looked at the bottom, they could see that the unglazed clay body had not been reduced. Nevertheless, the illusion was good enough for me. And over the years, I've had a number of people ask me for the recipe, which I've always been happy to give.

The recipe is actually a combination of two glazes that I mix in different proportions, depending on the result I want. One of them is called White Satin Matt, and the other is the one is called Nutmeg:

Most of the time, I mix the two glazes together in a ratio of two-thirds Nutmeg to one-third White Satin Matt. This gives me a light toasty color. For a darker, more quintessential wood-fired appearance, I decrease the proportion of White Satin Matt to about one-quarter or less.

On many of these pots, I also added some black brushwork. An oxide stain was applied with a long, thin brush made from deer bristles. This recipe was passed along to me by my former teacher, mentor and good friend, Sybil West.

To enhance the look of the black brushmarks, I first applied a fairly thick—roughly the consistency of heavy cream—swash of White Satin Matt over the main glaze combo, using a wide brush. This lightened the area behind the black, and made the brushwork really pop out.

I also discovered that I could alter the surface texture by varying the kiln temperature. Pots fired to about cone 5 tended to produce a drier surface, while those fired to cone 7, or even a little higher, came out with a shinier, more salted appearance.

I would encourage anyone who wants a wood/salt look from cone 6 oxidation firings to experiment a bit with kiln temperatures and with layered glazes. With a few tweaks here and there to adjust for your own kiln and firing techniques, you'll likely find a combination of color and texture that suits your taste to perfection. And who knows, you might even wind up fooling your friends in to thinking you're actually firing with wood and salt—at least at first glance.

CAUTION

Health risks are associated with metal oxides, particularly manganese. Handle carefully and fire in a well-ventilated kiln.

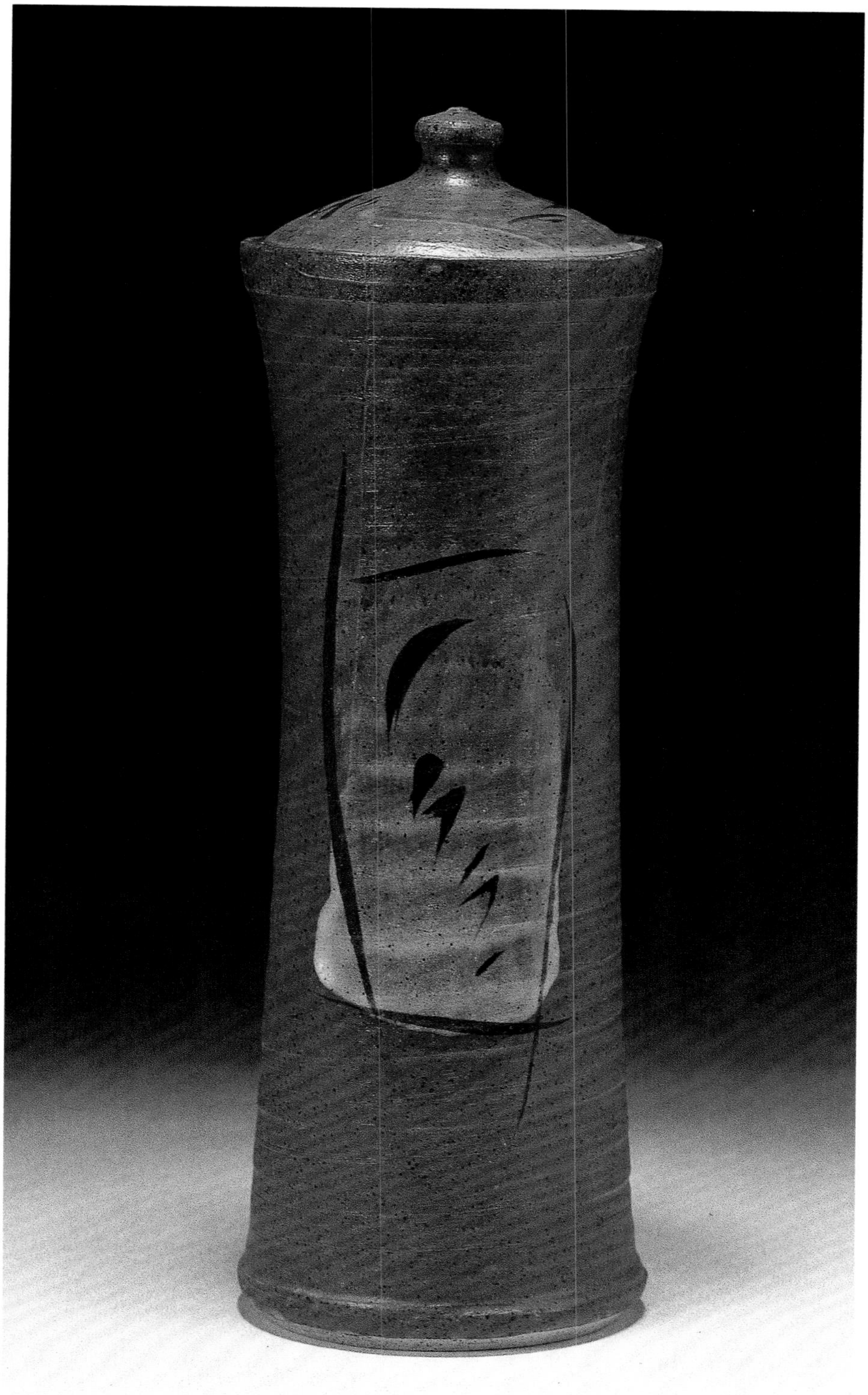

"Spaghetti Jar," 11¾ inches in height, stoneware, with stain and glazes, fired to cone 6.

Vase, 9 inches in height, faceted stoneware, with brush decoration on glaze, fired to cone 6 in an electric kiln, by Richard Busch.

Recipes

White Satin Matt Glaze

Cone 6

Gerstley Borate	31.6 %
Talc	14.0
Kona F-4 Feldspar	19.8
EPK Kaolin	5.0
Silica	29.6
	100.0 %
Add: Zircopax	5.1 %
Bentonite	2.0 %

Nutmeg Glaze

Cone 6

Dolomite	23.3 %
Spodumene	23.3
Ferro Frit 3134	6.8
Kentucky OM 4 Ball Clay	23.3
Silica	23.3
	100.0 %
Add: Red Iron Oxide	1.1 %
Yellow Ocher	3.2 %
Tin Oxide	4.8 %
Bentonite	2.0 %

Sybil's Black Stain

Black Copper Oxide	24.0 %
Cobalt Oxide	2.0
Manganese Dioxide	49.0
Nickel Oxide	5.0
Red Iron Oxide	20.0
	100.0 %

Adding Depth to Your Glazes

by Lisa Bare Culp

"Fish Bowl," matt white glaze over commercial glazes, fired to cone 6.

As a potter and in-home instructor for many years, I've always mixed my own glazes, or relied on other professionals who mix dry glazes to my specifications. Recently, an idea for a single pot challenged me to experiment with commercially-made glazes. The outcome has been succesful with vibrant new color selections, time savings and the convenience of readily available glazes screened for toxicity—all this without compromising my workspace or my standards.

What changed my thinking on commercially prepared glazes was my desire to introduce bold new colors into my work. I envisioned a piece with contrasting matt black-and-white slip surfaces offset against a single area glazed in vibrant red. My local supplier recommended a food-safe, nontoxic red glaze, Mayco's Stroke & Coat Cone 06.

Early Experiments

Early tests resulted in pieces with dramatic and beautiful contrasts between my porcelain slips and the red glaze. In one test, I used Stroke & Coat SC-73 Candy Apple Red, to highlight areas of bisqueware. In another, I used SC-74 Hot Tamale. Sometimes I applied the glaze with a big brush in a single, expressive stroke. Other times, I squeezed the colors from a slip trailer and a turkey baster.

After these loose applications, I dipped the entire piece in my usual cone 6 glazes. Because of their gum content, the commercial glazes resisted my glazes slightly, making the bold strokes of color come through vividly. Stroke edges were blended and their colors softly striking against the cone 6 palette. The outcome was as satisfying technically as it was aesthetically; I was satisfied with the melt (Stroke & Coat is a glaze, not an underglaze), the color and the absence of pinholing or other major flaws at cone 6.

A New Tool

Further experiments with sgraffito, layering, mixing with slip and stoneware glazes, and multiple firings have opened up commercial glazes as a new artistic tool—albeit an unexpected one—to share with students. They have learned the importance of experimenting with new surfaces, new materials, combining techniques and achieving balance with different kinds of material.

If you'd like to experiment with commercially prepared glazes, I've included three of my projects for you to try. Mixing my own recipes will always be an important part of understanding the science behind the art of pottery making. But successfully integrating commercial glazes in the mix is just one more way to pursue the function and beauty of ceramics.

Asparagus Tray

Pouring

Squeeze a large amount of Stroke & Coat SC-73 Candy Apple Red across the interior of a bisque-fired bowl. Use a 2-inch brush to apply a thin coat of Mayco's Elements Chunkies EL 203 Coal Dust (this is a low-fire effect glaze with crystals) over the Candy Apple Red.

A nice feathered edge is created when the piece is dipped into a cone 6 black glossy glaze.

Fish Bowl

Carving

Apply a thick coat of Mayco Stroke & Coat SC-71 Purple-Licious and SC-74 Hot Tamale with a large brush to the interior surface of a leather-hard bowl. Once the colors are slightly dry, the design is carved through the glaze with a loop tool, then bisque fired to cone 08. Dip the entire piece twice in a cone 6 matt white glaze and fire to cone 6 in oxidation. The commercial colors show well through the white matt.

Note: If the carved lines are too fine they may fill in when the glaze melts.

Gear Dish

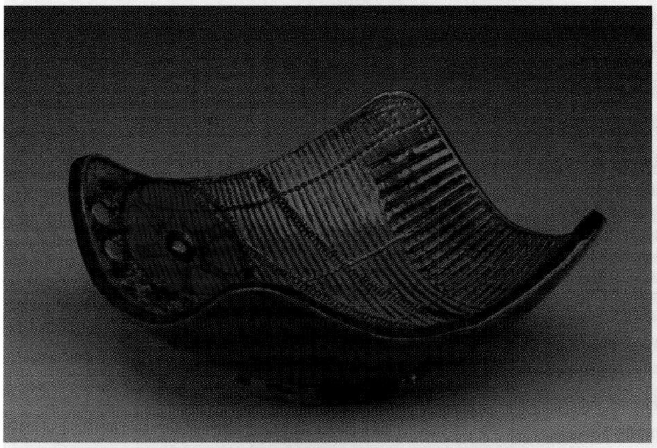

"Gear Dish," slab-built stoneware.

Layering

On a heavily textured, bisque-fired piece, apply a cone 6 porcelain black slip as a stain, wiping off the high spots with a damp sponge.

Use a 2-inch brush to apply Stroke & Coat SC-71 Purple-Licious to the high spots with a dry brush technique. Next, dry brush Mayco's Stroke & Coat Red SC-74 Hot Tamale and SC-27 Sour Apple onto the interior. Apply a thick coat of the red glaze in isolated areas to obtain a bright color.

Apply wax resist to the interior surface of the piece and allow to dry. Dip the entire piece in a cone 6 blue glaze.

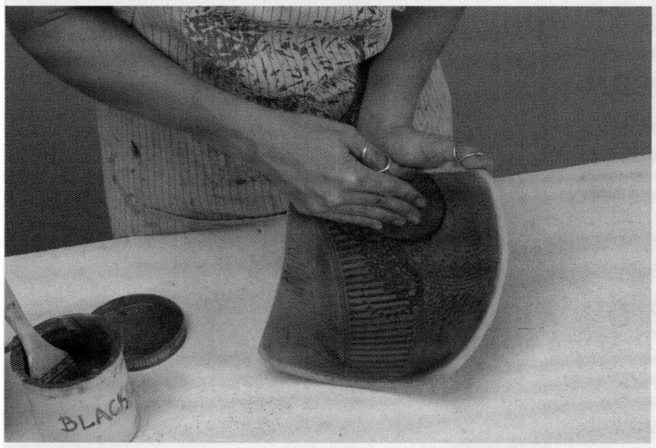

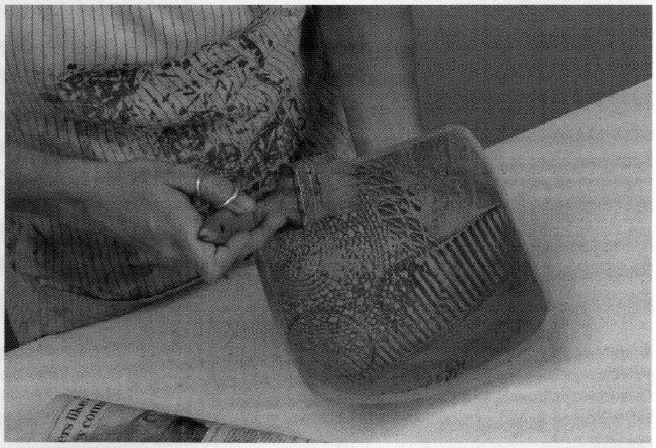

Kiln Firing Chart

Firing converts ceramic work from weak greenware into a strong, durable permanent form. As the temperature in a kiln rises, many changes take place at different temperatures and understanding what happens during the firng can help you avoid problems with a variety of clay and glaze faults related to firing.

Temperature °C	Temperature °F	Cone (approx.)	Incandescence	Event
1400	2552	14, 13, 12, 11	Brilliant white	End of porcelain range.
1300	2372	10, 9, 8, 7, 6	White; Yellow-white	End of stoneware range.
1200	2192	5, 4, 3, 2, 01, 02	Yellow	End of earthenware (red clay) range.
1100	2012	03, 04, 05	Yellow-orange; Orange	1100–1200°C: Mullite and cristobalite (two types of silica) form as clay begins to convert to glass. Particles start melting together to form crystals, and materials shrink as they become more dense. Soaking (holding the end temperature) increases the amount of fused material and the amount of chemical action between the fluxes and the more refractory materials.
1000	1832	06, 07, 08, 09, 010	Red-orange	
900	1652	011, 012, 013, 014, 015	Cherry red	800–900°C: the beginning of sintering, the stage where clay particles begin to cement themselves together to create a hard material called bisque.
800	1472	016, 017, 018	Dull red	300–800°C: Carbonaceous materials (impurities in the clay along with paper, wax, etc.) burn out. The kiln requires ample air during this stage since after 800°C sintering begins and the clay surface begins to seal off, trapping unburned materials and sulfides, which can cause bloating and black coring.
700	1292	019, 020, 021	Dark red	
600	1112	022		
500	932		Dull red glow; Black	573°C: Quartz inversion occurs where the quartz crystals change from an alpha (α) structure to a beta (β) structure. The inversion is reversed on cooling. This conversion creates stressses in the clay so temperature changes must be slow to avoid cracking the work.
400	752			Between 480–700°C chemical water ("water smoke") is driven off.
300	572			
200	392			Upon cooling, cristobalite, a crystalline form of silica found in all clay bodies, shrinks suddenly at 220°C. Fast cooling at this temperature causes ware to crack.
100	212			Water boils and converts to steam at 100°C. Trapped water causes clay to explode so keep the kiln below 100°C until all water has evaporated.